IMAGES
of America

REMEMBERING
MARSHALL FIELD'S

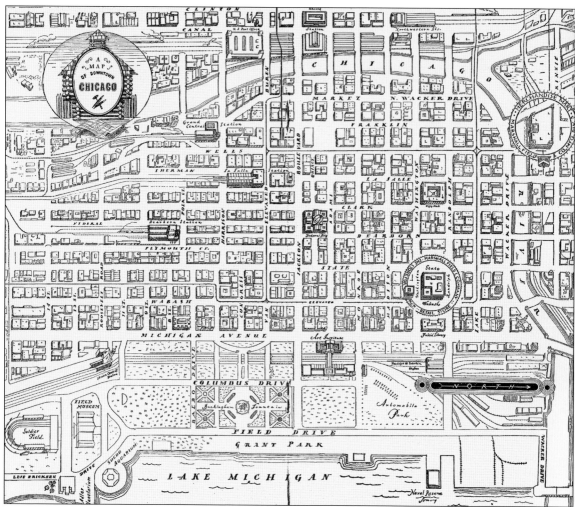

Marshall Field & Company's retail store (center right, circled) stood at the nucleus of Chicago's booming downtown Loop district in 1946. At this point, the 94-year-old company was the biggest department store in the Midwest and as famous nationally as Chicago's stockyards. The company no longer owned the Merchandise Mart (upper right, also circled), but still maintained space there for merchandise from its manufacturing division. (Author's collection.)

ON THE COVER: A bustling crowd converges outside Marshall Field & Company during the holiday season of 1938. At this point, the store had 234 selling sections, 45 passenger elevators, and 7,500 employees serving 65,000 customers daily (up to 200,000 on special occasions). Together, the 13-story main building, along with the six-story Store for Men on an adjacent corner covered approximately one-and-a-quarter city blocks with just over 61 acres of retail floor space. (Courtesy Chicago History Museum, ICHi-59534.)

IMAGES
of America

REMEMBERING
MARSHALL FIELD'S

Leslie Goddard

ARCADIA
PUBLISHING

Published by Arcadia Publishing
Charleston, South Carolina

Printed in the United States of America

Library of Congress Control Number: 2010939829

For all general information, please contact Arcadia Publishing:
Telephone 843-853-2070
Fax 843-853-0044
E-mail sales@arcadiapublishing.com
For customer service and orders:
Toll-Free 1-888-313-2665

Visit us on the Internet at www.arcadiapublishing.com

To Douma and Boppa, who introduced me to Marshall Field's; to Meme, who made that love a family tradition; and to Bruce, my dearest friend

CONTENTS

ACKNOWLEDGMENTS

When dealing with a department store that existed for 153 years, employed thousands, and sold to millions, the challenge is sifting through thousands upon thousands of photographs, advertisements, promotional items, and personal memories. In the case of Marshall Field's, a store that inspired passionate devotion, the chore is that much more challenging—and rewarding.

I am indebted to the Chicago History Museum (CHM), whose collections include a vast quantity of Marshall Field's materials. Without the assistance of CHM staffers, including Lesley Martin, Erin Tikovitsch, Elizabeth Reilly, and Leah Recht, this book would not have been possible—for their help I am immensely grateful.

Collections at other archives, libraries, and companies enrich our understanding of this remarkable store. Special thanks go to Morag Walsh and Sarah Zimmerman at the Chicago Public Library, Danielle N. Kramer at the Ryerson and Burnham Libraries at the Art Institute of Chicago, Jane Nicoll at the Park Forest Historical Society, Jane Rozek at the Schaumburg Township District Library, Lori Osborne and Eden Juron Pearlman at the Evanston History Center, Pat Barch at the Hoffman Estates Museum, Dave Gregoire at Those Funny Little People Enterprises, Inc., Deanna Boss at the Maccabee Group, and Nancy Wilson at the Elmhurst Historical Museum.

Many individuals made this book possible by digging through their own photograph albums and indulging me in long conversations about the past. Thank you for generously sharing your memories with us.

I also need to thank Melissa Basilone, my talented and supportive editor at Arcadia Publishing, and John Pearson, Arcadia's Midwest publisher. Ann Wendell, whose history of Frederick & Nelson inspired me, generously shared advice that steered my course.

My mother, Carol Goddard, and my sister, Laura Amann, provided early encouragement and steadfast support, while my nieces Elizabeth, Caroline, and Anna renewed my love for the Walnut Room, willingly helped with photographs, and listened to endless stories. Finally, to my husband, Bruce Allardice, thank you from the bottom of my heart for your expert guidance and your dogged encouragement, without which this book would not have been possible.

Where not otherwise indicated, images are from the author's collection.

INTRODUCTION

In the pantheon of American department stores, few names loom larger than that of Marshall Field & Company. Macy's and Hudson's might have been bigger, and A.T. Stewart earlier, but few department stores could match Field's for elegance, quality, luxury, and service.

"When I was a little kid, I had this sense of awe whenever I went there," said cultural historian and author David Garrard Lowe. "And when the Field's van came to your house to deliver something, that was an event." Nearly everyone who grew up in the Chicago area in living memory went to see the Marshall Field's holiday windows at least once. The words *fourth-floor toy department* still ring magically in the ears of many Chicagoans, and the store's huge bronze clocks have been rendezvous spots for more than a century. For its entire history, the store's stately granite retail building with its four grand entrance columns required no large sign, just discrete plaques set into the corners.

What distinguished Marshall Field & Company from the dozens of other stores stretching up and down Chicago's State Street shopping district in its heyday? How did this retailer earn its place as Chicago's leading department store and one of the top merchandisers in the world?

To understand that, we must go back to 1852, a time when Chicago had barely 30,000 residents and Marshall Field, the teenage son of a farmer, was clerking at a dry goods store in rural Massachusetts, little dreaming of Chicago.

That year, however, a remarkable young New Yorker named Potter Palmer stepped off the train in Chicago. Amidst the muddy streets and ramshackle wooden buildings, Palmer saw opportunity. This vigorous city, despite its youth and rough edges, had energy, an exceptional location, and the potential to become the country's greatest mercantile hub. Palmer abandoned plans to head farther west and opened a dry goods business on Lake Street, then Chicago's leading commercial district.

Palmer instituted many policies for which Marshall Field's would become famous. Borrowing ideas from New York dry goods pioneer A.T. Stewart (who in turn borrowed from the Bon Marché in Paris), he set fixed prices on his goods, displayed merchandise attractively, undersold his competitors on selected items, and stocked his store with both modestly priced wares and luxury merchandise—fine silks, soft woolens, sturdy cottons, and lace goods. Most importantly, he accepted returns for any reason, at a time when most merchants refunded money only if the goods arrived damaged. Palmer did not invent the one-price, no-haggle system or the satisfaction guarantee, but he did make them fundamental to his business.

What began as a 20-by-160-foot, retail-only shop became, within 13 years, one of Chicago's leading wholesale and retail dry goods businesses. When Palmer decided to sell, he turned to two energetic young men at a competing dry goods firm: Marshall Field, who had arrived in Chicago in 1856, and finance wunderkind Levi Leiter. Field and Leiter took up the offer, and in 1865, the firm of Field, Palmer & Leiter was launched. Palmer and his brother Milton stayed on as partners.

While the economic conditions of the postwar years tested the young company, Marshall Field and Levi Leiter were able to buy out the Palmers in 1867 and reorganize as Field, Leiter & Company. The partners continued many policies, especially the targeting of the wives and daughters of Chicago's newly wealthy. Field moved to New York City so he could oversee purchasing, selecting stylish products to appeal to those prosperous customers who were known as the "carriage trade."

Palmer now turned his attention to real estate, determined to relocate Chicago's commerce to State Street. In 1868, he convinced Marshall Field and Levi Leiter to move into his new six-story, marble-front building at the corner of State and Washington Streets. The larger, grander premises suited the partners' growing image, and they accepted.

Just three years later, the Great Chicago Fire of October 1871 swept through downtown Chicago, devastating thousands of businesses. Despite frantic efforts to save the Field, Leiter & Company building by flooding its sides with water and hanging wet blankets from the windows, the fire destroyed the building and everything not rescued from it. Determined to be among the first to reopen, Marshall Field and Levi Leiter resumed operations within three weeks in a former barn at State and 20th Streets, just outside the burnt district.

On the second anniversary of the fire, Field, Leiter & Company reopened retail operations in a lavish new building at their former site on State Street. The firm's business grew steadily as the population of the Midwest increased, and thousands of merchants opened for business. The keystones of the firm's success were now established: attentive service, quality merchandise, and dependably fashionable goods. As Chicago solidified its status as the mercantile, transportation, and financial hub of the Midwest, Marshall Field and Levi Leiter were key players in the commercial action.

Another devastating fire in 1877 destroyed the Field & Leiter retail store. Again, the partners reopened quickly, first in a former exposition building near the lakefront, and then, in April 1879, in a new structure at their former location on State Street.

This elegant French Renaissance building featured a mansard roof crowned by eight cupolas and a sun-drenched light well. Shopping here was a pleasurable experience, thanks to the elegance and the satisfaction guarantee, which lessened the need for clerks to use aggressive sales tactics. The firm issued employee rules, insisting that clerks "be polite and attentive to rich and poor alike . . . have patience in serving customers . . . [and] never misrepresent any article."

In 1881, Field convinced Leiter to retire and renamed the business Marshall Field & Company. He continued to emphasize service and quality goods and sought out exceptional workers, such as John G. Shedd, who began as a stock boy and rose to head of the wholesale division. Another eager employee named Harry Selfridge transformed the retail store into a full-fledged department store with 150 departments. Selfridge expanded a small, low-price basement department into a complete bargain basement (later renamed the "budget floor") in 1885, long before the concept took hold in other department stores.

Chicago's population soared, reaching 1.1 million by 1890. By 1900, the firm had offices in Britain, Germany, France, Belgium, and Japan, overseeing the importation of huge quantities of international goods. For customers of modest means, the firm offered "modifications" of European-styled merchandise. The firm also contracted with manufacturers to produce goods under the Field's label and sought exclusive distribution rights with specific makers. In the 1880s, Field's became the sole US distributor of Alexandre kid gloves from Paris. Selfridge worked out exclusive western rights to distribute goods from British painter William Morris. Whatever their economic situation, customers could be assured that purchasing from Field's meant reliable goods that reflected established standards of taste.

When Field died in 1906, his company was firmly established as a top-tier department store and world-class wholesale merchandiser. Pundits hailed him as one of the greatest merchants in American history.

At the time, the retail store was halfway through a rebuilding project that would make it, briefly, the largest department store in the world. When the massive building project ended in 1907, the store's frontage extended a full block along State Street.

Heralded with a weeklong celebration, the 13-story new store was striking both in size and in appearance. Clean-lined and modern, it boasted two-story granite columns and 76 elevators. Visitors gazed in awe at the south rotunda, which was topped with a vaulted, glass-mosaic ceiling designed by Louis Comfort Tiffany. Expansive plate-glass windows stretched down State Street. Talented window dresser Arthur Fraser took full advantage of these, using a lavish budget and a flair for abstract design to create arresting displays that drew worldwide attention.

The store's services now included waiting and resting rooms with comfortable chairs, an infirmary staffed by a trained nurse, and well-appointed lavatories. Customers could book a hotel room, purchase theater tickets, leave messages for friends, send telegrams, and look up train and bus schedules. The store had phone books from 100 American cities, a check-cashing bureau, a travel service, and a post office.

Still, the store had not finished growing. By 1914, expansions enabled it to occupy the entire block—and more after the Store for Men opened across the street from the main building at the southwest corner of Washington Street and Wabash Avenue.

Marshall Field & Company was not known as an innovator, but there were a few notable exceptions. In addition to the bargain basement, other firsts included the first department-store wedding registry, launched in 1924 as part of a larger gift registry service, and the first author book-signing, pioneered by the store's legendary book department in 1914.

More typically, the store monitored innovations at other stores and then instituted them in bigger, better, more elegant fashion. Marshall Field & Company was not the first department store to have a restaurant (Wanamaker's in Philadelphia and Macy's in New York both had restaurants by the late 1870s), or even the first in Chicago (The Fair began serving meals in 1885), but its tearooms outdid them in elegance and quality. Similarly, the store eschewed escalators for decades, long after low-priced department stores habitually installed them. When Field's finally did put in escalators, they were sleek, modern, double-wide versions.

By the 1920s, sales at Marshall Field's exceeded those of any department store in the world, and Chicagoans, if asked to name the top wonders of their city, would surely have included Field's in the top three. The company set the trends for fashion in Chicago and, through its wholesale division, the entire Midwest. As the automobile moved customers away from downtown, the firm followed, opening suburban branches in 1928 and 1929 in Lake Forest, Oak Park, and Evanston. In 1929, the company purchased Frederick & Nelson, Seattle's premier department store. Not neglecting those with more modest budgets, in 1923, Field's opened the discount Davis Store in the former home of A.M. Rothschild & Company at State Street and Jackson Boulevard.

With Frederick & Nelson came the Frango, the trademark for a future legend. Developed in 1918, the name originally referred to a maple-flavored dessert and in that form first appeared on Field's menus. But eventually the name was applied to a chocolate-mint bonbon that soared to fame. Starting in the late 1940s, the store aggressively promoted Frango mints as an iconic symbol of Marshall Field's.

Despite retail's success, wholesale had stopped growing and by the 1920s was on a precipitous decline. Leadership attempted to save its crown jewel by investing in a massive new structure called the Merchandise Mart that opened to great fanfare in 1930 and, sadly, did virtually nothing to stop the decline. Wholesale posted a staggering $8 million loss in 1932. On the advice of rapidly hired efficiency experts, store executives began slashing wholesale departments. By 1936, virtually all wholesale operations were gone, as was the Davis Store, sold to Goldblatt's.

The retail store, however, weathered the Great Depression and emerged in the 1940s stronger than ever. In 1941, the store solidified its status as Chicago's home for haute couture when it opened the 28 Shop, an exclusive high-fashion boutique within the store that boasted its own entrance and glamorous decor created by a Hollywood set designer.

The store's reputation for service now reached legendary proportions. One man regularly left alimony checks for his ex-wife at the Personal Service desk. Another asked the store to retrieve a package forgotten on a streetcar. A Denver man asked the store to find the address of a friend who had moved to Chicago.

Chicago's suburbs swelled in the postwar era, and Marshall Field's followed, opening a string of stores in suburban shopping malls throughout the 1950s, 1960s, and 1970s. The firm partially developed some of these, including Old Orchard in Skokie (opened 1956) and Oakbrook Center in Oak Brook (1962).

By this point, Chicagoans had developed strong emotional bonds to the store. For many, regularly priced items from Field's were symbols of social achievement. The store continued its long-standing tradition of offering prestige pieces—costly items such as a set of 24-karat-gold-plated golf clubs offered for $2,500 in 1979—that served mostly to bolster the store's image.

Still, even Marshall Field's was not immune to pressures from the mass discounters and specialty retailers that exploded in numbers starting in the 1960s. The downtown store gradually chiseled away at services, eliminating the children's playroom, doormen, and other services. It cut back on custom work and eventually on free delivery for most items. Company executives opened four stores in Texas and acquired chains in North Carolina and Wisconsin. Scrambling to fend off an attempted takeover by corporate raider Carl Icahn, the board of directors sold the firm in 1982 to BATUS, Inc., a subsidiary of British American Tobacco, for $367 million.

The sale marked the end of Field's as an independent Chicago-based firm, but BATUS also brought new vision to the downtown store. Starting in 1987, BATUS embarked on a multimillion-dollar renovation that finally unified the State Street store's six buildings around a soaring central atrium.

In 1990, BATUS sold Marshall Field's to the Dayton Hudson Corporation (later Target Corporation) for $1.04 billion. Target, in turn, sold Field's in 2004 to the May Department Stores Company for $3.2 billion. May ceased to exist in 2005 when Federated Department Stores Incorporated (today Macy's Incorporated) acquired it. Not long after, Federated announced that more than 400 former May stores, including Marshall Field's, would be converted to the Macy's brand and renamed Macy's in September 2006.

Today, the Chicago downtown store operates as Macy's on State Street, one of four divisional flagship Macy's stores. The Marshall Field's heritage lives on in numerous legacies of the past: the bronze clocks, the Tiffany mosaic, the Walnut Room, the holiday windows, Frango mints, and more.

In a larger sense, Marshall Field left a legacy that goes far beyond the store itself. His firm helped transform a rough-and-tumble frontier town into one of the nation's premiere cities for business, culture, and art. Philanthropy from Field executives helped establish the Field Museum of Natural History (renamed in 1905 in honor of its first large benefactor), the John G. Shedd Aquarium, and the University of Chicago. State Street's era as one of the world's great shopping districts owes much to Marshall Field's, as indeed does Chicago's flourishing reputation as a leader in fashion retail and merchandising.

One

FROM P. PALMER TO FIELD & LEITER

(1852–1880)

The story of Marshall Field's begins with an energetic and visionary young Quaker from New York, Potter Palmer, who opened a small dry goods store at 137 Lake Street in 1852. Business was unremarkable at first, but Palmer introduced some advanced merchandising methods. He eliminated haggling over pricing, displayed luxury goods attractively, and accepted returns for any reason. (Courtesy Chicago History Museum/J. Carbutt, ICHi-27395.)

As business grew—and then flourished—Palmer expanded. By 1857, he had a wholesale division. In 1858, he moved into a five-story building at 112 Lake Street (center). The *Chicago Tribune* proclaimed it "one of the finest and most costly" buildings in the country. P. Palmer Dry Goods became Chicago's leading dry goods store, and Palmer himself became known as "The A.T. Stewart of the West," after the great New York merchant.

In 1856, John Farwell, senior partner at competing wholesale firm Cooley, Wadsworth & Company, noticed that the firm's new 22-year-old clerk from Conway, Massachusetts, regularly worked 14-hour days. Marshall Field showed amazing dedication and skill. "He could find out quicker what a woman wanted and sell her quicker than any other clerk," said Farwell. "He knew how to show off stock. . . . The store and the stock was his life."

Although quiet—even shy—and excruciatingly frugal, Marshall Field rose quickly. Within four years, he was a junior partner. In 1864, the firm reorganized as Farwell, Field & Company. When doctors advised Palmer to sell his business and go abroad for his health, Palmer approached Field and one of his coworkers, a bookkeeper and credit man named Levi Leiter. Leiter's flair for finances complemented Field's sales and merchandising skills.

Marshall Field and Levi Leiter joined forces and in 1865 launched the new firm of Field, Palmer & Leiter (The *Palmer* in the name probably stood for Milton Palmer, Potter's brother, who stayed on as retail manager). The firm weathered some challenges but soon found its feet. Within two years, Field and Leiter bought out the Palmers and changed the firm's name to Field, Leiter & Company. Marshall Field was just 33 years old.

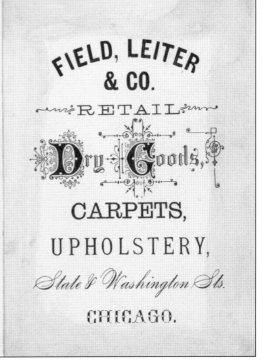

When Palmer's health recovered, he turned his attention to State Street. As part of his plan to shift Chicago's commercial district from Lake Street to cleaner, more expansive State Street, he built a six-story marble palace at the corner of State and Washington Streets and convinced Marshall Field and Levi Leiter to move their wholesale and retail operations into the grand new structure. Despite the staggering annual rent of $50,000, the partners saw the advantages and signed on. Over 10 nights, they moved their entire stock to the new marble-front building, which opened to great fanfare on the morning of October 12, 1868. Field and Leiter personally greeted the crowds of visitors who came to see their new store, giving each man a cigar and each woman a rose. The *Chicago Tribune* called it "the grandest affair of its kind which ever transpired in Chicago, the city of grand affairs."

Rockford Ill

FIELD, LEITER & CO.
WHOLESALE DRY GOODS, STATE & WASHINGTON STS

Chicago, Nov 26 1869

Received of Geo H. Dennett
Four hundred sixty five 27/100 ——— dollars
to bal bills Oct 26, 1869

  461.23 ch.
    4.04 dis.
$ 465 27/100

Tower, Millard & Decker, Stationers, Chicago.

Field, Leiter & Co.
by Ingraham

Dry-goods merchant George Dennett of Rockford probably traveled by railroad to Chicago in 1869 to select the goods for which he received this $465 receipt. Small, independent storekeepers such as Dennett sold some 90 percent of all retail merchandise in the United States in the mid- to late 19th century. The wholesale division of Field & Leiter served as a valuable clearinghouse (and warehouse) for Midwestern merchants and offered credit to reputable small stores.

After the Great Chicago Fire swept through Chicago's commercial district on October 8, 1871, nothing but rubble remained at State and Washington Streets. The fire destroyed the Field & Leiter building and more than $2 million of goods. Less than three weeks later, wholesale operations reopened in a former streetcar barn at State and 20th Streets, joined by the retail business one week after that. (Courtesy Chicago History Museum, ICHi-37113.)

FIELD, LEITER & CO.
WHOLESALE DEPARTMENT.

In March 1872, the firm's wholesale operations reopened in a new building at Madison and Market Streets. The neighborhood, formerly occupied by cheap boardinghouses and saloons, took on new character after the fire, thanks to its convenient location for buyers arriving at the city's railroad stations. For the first time, wholesale operated separately from retail—even though the retail store still bought most of its merchandise from the wholesale division.

On October 9, 1873, exactly two years after the fire, Field & Leiter's retail operations reopened on State and Washington Streets in a new structure that was one-third larger than the pre-fire building. This building, owned by the Singer Sewing Machine Company, stood five stories tall and had an ornate French Empire look. Its opulent appearance, spacious light wells, and elaborate gas chandeliers clearly signaled the store's magnificence to even the most uncultured out-of-town visitor.

Marshall Field and Levi Leiter regularly advertised in *Chicago Magazine*, the city's leading fashion publication. The store did not stock these dresses per se, but rather fabrics—bolts of silks, velvets, and woolens—along with ribbons and trimmings. Illustrations served as guides for women sewing their own clothing or working with a dressmaker. By 1877, the firm's 700 employees included dozens of dressmakers and fitters. (Courtesy Chicago History Museum, ICHi-61945.)

FASHIONS FOR MAY, 1874, FROM FIELD, LEITER & CO.

THE FIRE.

Field & Leiter's Great Retail Store Destroyed.

Loss on Building and Stock Will Reach About $1,200,000.

On Which There Is Insurance Amounting to About $1,100,000.

The Fire Broke Out Where It Did in 1873.

The Fault Being with That Same Inaccessible Half-Roof.

Various and Conflicting Statements About the Origin of the Blaze.

How the Firemen Fought It—Fall of the Blazing Roof.

On November 14, 1877, Field, Leiter & Company suffered another ruinous fire, this time from a defective chimney flue. The fire destroyed the building and $900,000 in merchandise. "It is doubtful," mused the *Chicago Tribune*, whether "the burning up of the Vatican could have excited such a keen local interest. . . . This was the place of worship of thousands of our female fellow-citizens." The store reopened temporarily in a lakefront exposition building.

17

L. Z. Leiter

In 1879, Singer completed a new six-story building (seen here in the 1890s), but Levi Leiter initially balked at the $700,000 price. While Marshall Field and Levi Leiter bickered, Singer announced it would be leased to the competing firm of Carson, Pirie & Company. Field and Leiter ultimately paid the $700,000—plus an additional $100,000 for the broken lease. (Courtesy Chicago Public Library, Special Collections and Preservation Division, Chicago City-Wide Collection 62/4, plate 1.)

With his burly beard and piercing eyes, Levi Leiter had looks to match his irascible personality. His firm financial oversight kept the company on solid footing, but he also alienated many. He was known to deny goods to a cash customer simply because he disapproved of the man's reputation—or looks. Relations between the partners frayed as Field's enthusiasm grew for transforming State Street into an incomparable shopping district. (Courtesy Chicago History Museum/W.G. Phillips, ICHi-62365.)

Two

MARSHALL FIELD &
COMPANY EMERGES
(1881–1906)

Marshall Field bought out Levi Leiter in 1881
and changed the firm's name to Marshall Field
& Company. Like most retail establishments,
the company distributed lithographed trade
cards at the door and by mail to customers, who
collected them in albums. Note that this card
does not display anything one might actually
purchase at the store. Rather, it associates Field's
with a pleasant image of fantasy and beauty.

In 1887, the firm opened a new wholesale building that covered the city block bounded by Adams, Quincy, Wells (then Fifth), and Franklin Streets. Designed by architect Henry Hobson Richardson and built in the era before concrete, steel, and glass developed, the rugged structure lacked any exterior ornamentation, but managed to convey a forceful, authoritative presence. Although now recognized as a milestone in American architecture, the building was demolished in 1930.

As this letterhead shows, by 1891 the firm had buying offices in Great Britain (opened by Marshall's brother Joseph Field in 1871), Paris, and Germany. By 1906, Marshall Field's would be the country's largest importer, purchasing $6 million in foreign goods annually. International offices ensured quick dispatches to Chicago, and because the wholesale house supplied goods for the retail store, retail customers had prompt access to the latest, choicest styles.

By the 1890s, a number of expensive and prestigious dry goods houses—including Marshall Field & Company (center right, with clock)—spanned what was known as the "Ladies Half Mile" between Randolph and Adams Streets. Below them, popularly priced department stores stretched south to Congress Street. Less than 15 years after its grand opening, the French Renaissance building that housed Marshall Field's no longer stood out—its once-dominating architectural elegance and size had become commonplace.

Confident, innovative, and bursting with ideas, Harry Gordon Selfridge hauled the retail store into the modern era. Hired as a wholesale stock boy in 1879, he rose to director of retail operations by 1887. Selfridge worked tirelessly, tripling the number of telephones, inaugurating annual sales, and expanding nearly everything. "Mile-a-Minute Harry" left the firm in 1904 and eventually opened Selfridge's Department Store in London. (Courtesy Chicago History Museum/S. Langfrier, ICHi-62399.)

In 1892, Harry Selfridge convinced Marshall Field to commission a new building to accommodate the many visitors coming to Chicago for the World's Columbian Exposition. The nine-story annex built at the northwest corner of Wabash Avenue and Washington Street dazzled visitors when it opened in August 1893. Chief designer Charles B. Atwood of D.H. Burnham & Company equipped it with 13 high-pressure hydraulic elevators, hand-carved mahogany counters, and modern lavatories. The lower three floors were dedicated to selling, with workrooms and rental office space above. The annex added 100,000 square feet to the company's sales space, bringing its total retail sales space to nine acres. Not everyone, though, was impressed. Architect Louis Sullivan probably was referring to this building in his scathing criticism of urban buildings that failed to convey architecturally their mercantile purpose. (Courtesy Library of Congress, Prints and Photographs Division, LC-USZ62-61681.)

For the October 1892 dedication of the World's Columbian Exposition, Harry Selfridge lavished $10,000 on decorations for the retail store. During the run of the fair (May through October 1893), he made Field's an attraction in itself. "Our retail store," read one advertisement, "is a continual and ever-changing exposition." To assist foreign visitors during the fair, the store hired interpreters and stationed them at the doors. (Courtesy Chicago History Museum, ICHi-62400.)

Selfridge talked Field into enlarging the advertising budget, often writing the exuberant copy himself. This advertisement from October 1893 trumpets the store as "one of the most noteworthy sights of the city," and praises the "wonderfully complete stocks." Like Field, Selfridge insisted on absolute accuracy. He later offered a one-dollar cash prize for any employee who found an advertisement containing an exaggeration, incorrect price, or misspelled word.

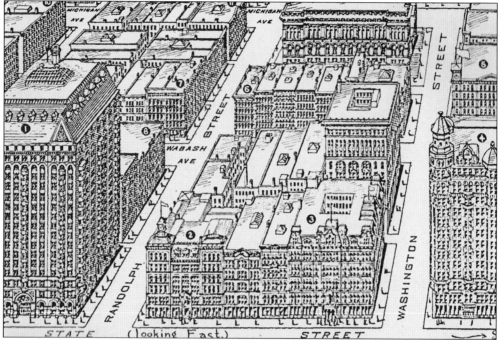

Look for the light well at the center of the older Marshall Field's building (marked 3) on this bird's-eye-view map from 1893. The limitations of gas light made natural light critical for a retail store in the late 19th century. Field's retained the concept of light wells in its future State Street buildings, even after most department stores abandoned them. The city library building (top center) still stands as the Chicago Cultural Center.

Full service ruled the store in the 1890s, as this photograph of the lace department shows. Customers sat or stood while clerks retrieved goods from drawers and tall cases. Parasols, handkerchiefs, and gloves were among the impulse goods positioned for high visibility on the first floor. (Courtesy Historic Architecture and Landscape Image Collection, Ryerson and Burnham Archives, Art Institute of Chicago, digital file No. 59981, © Art Institute of Chicago.).

Selfridge expanded not only the store's merchandise offerings, but also its services. The glove-cleaning department, seen here at left, was one of many services that also included jewelry and shoe repair, photograph developing, custom tailoring, and custom upholstery. Selfridge also convinced Field to expand and aggressively promote the basement saleroom. What had opened in 1879 as a basement salesroom for a lower-priced line of retail goods became, in 1885, a full-fledged low-priced budget department to attract customers who could not afford the store's higher-priced goods but still desired something from Field's. Selfridge's pioneering bargain basement would eventually become the largest single saleroom in the world, grossing $25 million annually. By the time Selfridge left in 1904, the retail store had 150 departments—a huge increase from 1883, when it boasted fewer than 50. (Courtesy Historic Architecture and Landscape Image Collection, Ryerson and Burnham Archives, Art Institute of Chicago, digital file No. 59982, © Art Institute of Chicago.)

Note the annex's light fixtures (seen here in the second-floor linen department). Marshall Field's was one of the first Chicago firms to install electric lights, with power supplied by two dynamos and a 75-horsepower engine in the basement. The store used electricity and gas together for a while, until gas finally was eliminated in 1902. (Courtesy Chicago Public Library, Special Collections and Preservation Division, Chicago City-Wide Collection 62/4, plate 12.)

Piles of stationery stand heaped on tables, making it simple for customers to browse without assistance. Selfridge constantly pushed to implement modern merchandising methods that would increase sales. He convinced Field to rip out counters and move goods from behind wooden cases onto tables or into glass-front displays. (Courtesy Historic Architecture and Landscape Image Collection, Ryerson and Burnham Archives, Art Institute of Chicago, digital file No. 59980, © Art Institute of Chicago.)

Several African Americans are visible in this view from 1895 taken just outside the store. Field's did not exclude anyone, but, like many department stores, had informal rules that kept non-white customers away or steered them to the basement. In 1929, a reporter for the *Chicago Defender* wrote, "One seldom finds a Colored person in the store, and never have I seen one on the upper floors." (Courtesy Chicago History Museum, ICHi-20239.)

Look in the upper right for the store's first corner clock, installed in 1897. Marshall Field allegedly ordered the clock after pedestrians began tucking notes to friends into the store's window frames. The clock quickly became a handy meeting place, giving rise to the phrase, "Meet me under the clock." People with no intention of shopping now had a reason to come to the store. (Courtesy Chicago History Museum, ICHi-01616.)

Around 1900, construction workers appeared on State Street tearing down the buildings closest to Randolph Street and beginning work on another new Marshall Field & Company building. To design the new building, Field again hired the architectural firm of Daniel Burnham, who was then riding a wave of world fame for overseeing construction of the World's Columbian Exposition. (Courtesy Chicago History Museum/E.C. Bunting, ICHi-62401.)

Colossal! Magnificent! Magical! The *Dry Goods Reporter* reached for superlatives in describing the new store (left, with columns), declaring it "an epoch-making event in the retail history of the world." More than two million people toured the store during its six-day opening celebration in fall 1902. Note that the 1879 building (right) has been remodeled. An expansion project in 1898 eliminated the mansard roof and added several new floors.

The 1902 store differed from any previous Field's store in one significant respect. Yard goods—the fabrics that had been fundamental to the store since its earliest days—now occupied the second floor. The move acknowledged a shift in merchandising, as ready-made women's clothing expanded and impulse items replaced necessities on the first floor. (Courtesy Chicago Public Library, Special Collections and Preservation Division, Chicago City-Wide Collection 62/4, plate 5.)

Field shrewdly invested in Chicago's expanding transportation system, helping ensure that streetcar and railroad lines ran near his store (center right). The elevated train ran along Lake Street at rear, and streetcars traveled down State Street at center. Another streetcar line one block west and a railroad terminal two blocks east brought more customers within easy reach. Store-operated omnibuses brought passengers from other railroad terminals right to the store.

The millinery department of the 1902 store included mirrors for checking one's appearance and dressing tables arranged so clerks could assist from behind. At the time, well-bred women changed hats to match the season and the social occasion. Often swathed in ribbons and towering with flowers and plumage, the hats were large, lavish, and visually enticing. (Courtesy Chicago Public Library, Special Collections and Preservation Division, Chicago City-Wide Collection 62/4, plate 14.)

Allegedly, a millinery saleswoman named Mrs. Hering one day offered her chicken pot pie to some hungry shoppers (at a time when few restaurants served unaccompanied women). Selfridge loved the idea and opened a 15-table tearoom in 1890. When the annex opened, a tearoom occupied its entire fourth floor. The tearoom of 1902 (seen here) was even larger. (Courtesy Chicago Public Library, Special Collections and Preservation Division, Chicago City-Wide Collection 62/4, plate 16.)

The new building had a second-floor women's suit department offering tailored, ready-to-wear suits that had recently become a sort of uniform for women in public. With inexpensive labor readily available from newly immigrated tailors and sewers, these suits sold for reasonable prices. Their popularity accelerated the shift in retail stores from yard goods to ready-to-wear clothing. (Courtesy Chicago Public Library, Special Collections and Preservation Division, Chicago City-Wide Collection 62/4, plate 6.)

Christmas shoppers in 1905 clutch packages wrapped in brown paper. For women in this era, shopping downtown typically meant maneuvering public transportation or horse-drawn carriages while keeping their sidewalk-sweeping skirts out of the dirt. As the store grew, and purchases increased, more and more shoppers requested that merchandise be delivered to their homes. (Courtesy Chicago History Museum, *Chicago Daily News* negatives collection, DN-0002536.)

Shopping by Telephone is a Most Convenient Way

"Private Exchange-One"

Marshall Field & Company's Telephone Switchboard, the largest private telephone system in the world. Over 250 branch lines. Requires fourteen day operators to make connections. A branch line runs to every section of the store.

There is a growing satisfaction in shopping by telephone with us. Every effort is being made to make it so. Every order, inquiry, or request will be quickly and intelligently cared for. Every section of this store is at your service.

Call for "Private Exchange-One," and then ask the operator for the section you wish to speak with. If in doubt, explain briefly to the operator, who will give proper connection. For directory of sections, see page 90.

Marshall Field & Company
State, Washington, Randolph and Wabash Ave.

Marshall Field & Company had the world's largest private telephone system by 1904, as this advertisement from the *Chicago 1904 Telephone Directory* announces. Telephone shopping helped Field's compete with the efficient mail-order catalogs such as Montgomery Ward & Company (founded 1872) and Sears, Roebuck & Company (founded 1886). "Private Exchange-One" later became the automatic number STate1-1000. By the 1920s, the store would be handling 29,000 calls daily. (Courtesy Chicago History Museum, ICHi-01614.)

Marshall Field—the third wealthiest citizen and possibly the largest individual taxpayer in the United States—died suddenly of pneumonia on January 16, 1906. The company immediately closed for three days. On the day of his funeral, stores along State Street closed, and Chicago flags flew at half-mast. He left most of his fortune, which had an estimated value of $100–$175 million, to grandsons Henry Field and Marshall Field III.

Three

RETAIL GROWS AND WHOLESALE DECLINES (1907–1945)

Soon after Marshall Field's death, wooden barriers went up at State and Washington Streets as the next phase of construction began. The new building would replace the structure from 1879, giving the retail store a unified frontage along State Street. This photograph, taken just after the old building was demolished, reveals the connecting bridges over Holden Court into the annex. (Courtesy Chicago History Museum, *Chicago Daily News* negatives collection, DN-0003889.)

The presidency of Marshall Field's now fell to John G. Shedd. Hired as a stock boy in 1872, Shedd quickly showed a flair for salesmanship. Eventually promoted to head of wholesale, he quadrupled the number of traveling salesmen, extended credit conscientiously, and saw annual wholesale revenues reach $20 million. Field once said, "I honestly believe that Mr. Shedd is the best merchant in America." (Courtesy Chicago History Museum, *Chicago Daily News* negatives collection, DN-0066830.)

In 1907, a weeklong celebration heralded the opening of a new building, which matched its 1902 partner and created a cohesive modern building. The white granite and steel walls made a neat grid across the front, and the windows were, as one admirer put it, "so numerous that the building seems a veritable palace of glass." (Courtesy Library of Congress, Prints and Photographs Division, Detroit Publishing Company Collection, LC-D4-34698.)

GRAPHIC DIRECTORY OF STATE STREET BUILDING

STATE STREET BUILDING

NORTH ROOM	MIDDLE ROOM	SOUTH ROOM	
FUR WORK ROOM	WORK ROOMS	12 ALTERATION ROOM FOR WOMEN'S GARMENTS	TWELFTH FLOOR
STOCK ROOMS	RECEIVING ROOMS	11 STOCK ROOMS, WORK ROOMS	ELEVENTH FLOOR
WORK ROOMS	EMPLOYES' LUNCH ROOM	10 EMPLOYES' REST ROOMS, WORK ROOMS	TENTH FLOOR
EXECUTIVE OFFICES	AUDITING AND MAIL ORDER	9 DRESSMAKING	NINTH FLOOR
TOYS	TRUNKS AND SPORTING GOODS	8 SPECIAL SALES EVENTS	EIGHTH FLOOR
GRILL ROOM	TEA ROOM	7 GRILL ROOM	SEVENTH FLOOR
WOMEN'S COATS, NEGLIGEES AND SACQUES	WAISTS	6 SUITS, COSTUMES, TAILORED SKIRTS	SIXTH FLOOR
FURS, MILLINERY	MILLINERY	5 UNDERWEAR, CORSETS, AND PETTICOATS	FIFTH FLOOR
BOYS' CLOTHING AND FURNISHINGS	GIRLS' CLOTHING AND FURNISHINGS	4 HOSIERY, SHOES, INFANTS' WEAR	FOURTH FLOOR
WAITING ROOM	COUNTING ROOM	3 LINENS, DOMESTIC COTTONS, QUILTS, BLANKETS, FANCY GOODS	THIRD FLOOR
MEN'S CLOTHING	WHITE GOODS, COLORED WASH GOODS, PATTERNS	2 DRESS GOODS, LACE ROBES, SILKS, VELVETS, FLANNELS	SECOND FLOOR
MEN'S FURNISHINGS	NOTIONS, PERFUMES, RIBBONS	1 LACES, HANDKERCHIEFS, EMBROIDERIES, UMBRELLAS, BUTTONS, WOMEN'S NECKWEAR, DRESS TRIMMINGS, GLOVES	FIRST FLOOR
THE GREAT	BASEMENT		
	PURCHASE TICKET DIVISION	SALESROOM	FIRST BASEMENT
	SUBWAY	EMPLOYES' LOCKERS	SECOND BASEMENT
		VENTILATING FANS, WAREHOUSING, MACHINERY	THIRD BASEMENT

GRAPHIC DIRECTORY OF STATE STREET BUILDING

The store booklet from 1907, *Marshall Field & Company: The World's Greatest Merchandisers*, included diagrams showing the array of departments. Some—such as the restaurants on the seventh floor—would never leave their 1907 locations. Others, including toys on the eighth floor, would move. On the first floor, customers could purchase jewelry and perfumes, but not cosmetics; makeup as it is known today would not become commonplace until after World War I.

The Wabash Avenue building (which did not yet extend the entire block to Randolph Street) already had departments for cameras, motor accessories, and photographic supplies. The fourth-floor Oak Room sold classic furniture, while the Hotel Bureau on the third floor handled contract work outfitting hotels, clubs, hospitals, and even boats and railroad cars.

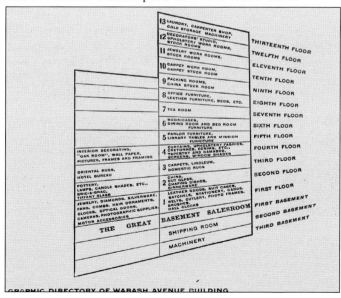

	13 LAUNDRY, CARPENTER SHOP, COLD STORAGE MACHINERY	THIRTEENTH FLOOR
	12 DECORATORS' STUDIO, UPHOLSTERY WORK ROOMS, STOCK ROOMS	TWELFTH FLOOR
	11 JEWELRY WORK ROOMS, STOCK ROOMS	ELEVENTH FLOOR
	10 CARPET WORK ROOM, CARPET STOCK ROOM	TENTH FLOOR
	9 PACKING ROOMS, CHINA STOCK ROOM	NINTH FLOOR
	8 OFFICE FURNITURE, LEATHER FURNITURE, BEDS, ETC.	EIGHTH FLOOR
	7 TEA ROOM	SEVENTH FLOOR
	6 BOOK-CASES, DINING ROOM AND BED ROOM FURNITURE	SIXTH FLOOR
	5 PARLOR FURNITURE, LIBRARY TABLES AND MISSION FURNITURE	FIFTH FLOOR
INTERIOR DECORATING, "OAK ROOM", WALL PAPER, PICTURES, FRAMES AND FRAMING	4 CURTAINS, UPHOLSTERY FABRICS, CRETONNES, DENIMS, ETC., TAPESTRY AND DAMASKS, SCREENS, WINDOW SHADES	FOURTH FLOOR
ORIENTAL RUGS, HOTEL BUREAU	3 CARPETS, LINOLEUM, DOMESTIC RUGS	THIRD FLOOR
POTTERY, LAMPS, CANDLE SHADES, ETC., BRIC-A-BRAC, TIFFANY GLASS, JEWELRY, DIAMONDS, SILVERWARE, FANS, COMBS, HAIR ORNAMENTS, CLOCKS, OPTICAL GOODS, CAMERAS, PHOTOGRAPHIC SUPPLIES, MOTOR ACCESSORIES	2 CHINA, CUT GLASS, CHAFING DISHES, DINNERWARE, LEATHER GOODS, SUIT CASES, SATCHELS, STATIONERY, CARDS, BELTS, CUTLERY, PHOTO FRAMES, BRUSHES, HALL CLOCKS	FIRST FLOOR
THE GREAT	BASEMENT SALESROOM	FIRST BASEMENT
	SHIPPING ROOM	SECOND BASEMENT
	MACHINERY	THIRD BASEMENT

GRAPHIC DIRECTORY OF WABASH AVENUE BUILDING

Innovative window dresser Arthur Fraser rejected traditional merchandise-heavy displays in favor of artistic creations with modern abstract designs, such as this sleek showcase from around 1910. Discovered by Selfridge while working in an Iowa store, Fraser reigned over the Field's windows for 49 years. New technology had made vast plate-glass windows possible, and Fraser filled them with visual extravaganzas. In 1922 *The Show Window* dubbed him "America's foremost artist in window display."

The company's concern with character, a vestige of Marshall Field's New England Calvinist upbringing, extended even to the windows. The shirred curtains, visible at top left in this 1910 photograph, were lowered at closing on Saturdays and not raised until Monday mornings. Similarly, until 1934, the firm almost never advertised in Sunday newspapers. In the company's view, a respectable reputation in the community was key to strong sales. (Courtesy Chicago History Museum, Chicago Daily News, DN-008625.)

The building's overall bulk conveyed the company's desired image of solidity and reputability, while its clean lines spoke to its modernity. The white granite exterior gleamed among the city's dark brownstone and red brick, at least until it acquired layers of grime from Chicago's sooty air. Pierce Anderson, then chief designer for D.H. Burnham & Company, planned the store with its main entrance in the middle to permit easy access to the main floor's grand aisles. Customers, however, found it awkward to stop carriages there. Eventually the store converted most of its original elegant vestibule into selling space. (Courtesy Library of Congress, Prints and Photographs Division, Detroit Publishing Company Collection, LC-D4-34699.)

The four Ionic columns now stood at the center of an architecturally unified building. It was said that only the 70-foot-high columns of Egypt's Temple of Karnak surpassed these massive granite columns, which towered almost 49 feet above the streets of Chicago. Other columns lined the top-floor loggia and interior main aisle, contributing to an overall statement of strength and endurance. (Courtesy Library of Congress, Prints and Photographs Division, Detroit Publishing Company Collection/Hans Behm, LC-D4-34700.)

In 1907, a new clock replaced the original at State and Washington Streets. Pierce Anderson designed the massive clock and its identical partner at State and Randolph Streets (installed in 1902). The clocks each stand 17.5 feet above the sidewalk and, like the lions at the Art Institute of Chicago, have become icons of the store and of Chicago.

The two clocks emerge from the store's corners like prows of a battleship. Each made from seven and three-quarter tons of cast bronze (giving them a soft-green patina), they have clock faces measuring 46 inches across. Their minute hands are 27 inches long, and their hour hands are 20.5 inches long. Note that four o'clock is indicated by *IIII* instead of the standard *IV*, probably to avoid confusion with *VI*. (Courtesy Greg McAfee, fotolia.com.)

Elaborate decorations adorned the store's wide main aisle for special occasions. Corinthian columns drew the eye down the aisle's 385-foot-long expanse, emphasizing the sweeping, dramatic expanse of space. The sleek, rounded-end mahogany counters were reportedly devised by Shedd himself. The store generally preferred fixtures in mahogany, although other woods were used if they provided the desired look of "rarest effects in paneling and molding."

The building's masterpiece was the vaulted, Louis Comfort Tiffany mosaic ceiling in the south rotunda, seen here in a modern photograph. The installation of 1.6 million pieces of iridescent glass reportedly took 50 men two years to complete. The world's biggest glass mosaic, it attracted so many admirers at its unveiling in September 1907 that Shedd worried the floor beneath might buckle. One critic described it as "in a class with the nave of St. Peter in Rome."

This image of the second-floor cloak department reveals the store's early upper-floor decor. Above the first floor, all the sales floors had rich, deep-toned carpeting and an abundance of plants. Only a few pieces of merchandise were displayed. In most cases, customers still stood or sat while a model displayed choice merchandise or a clerk brought out a few selected items. The north light well is visible to the left.

Customers could relax in the comfortable reading, writing, and waiting rooms covering the third floor's north end. Women and men enjoyed separate waiting rooms, while weary shoppers could nap in wicker rocking chairs or couches in the silence room. The reading room had "all standard magazines," all Chicago newspapers, and all large city newspapers and city directories.

The services provided by Marshall Field's became legendary. By the 1920s, shoppers could buy theater tickets, send telegrams, and purchase stamps and send packages at a postal station. They could also order cabs and check the arrival and departure times of trains, steamers, and street railways. Once, when a railroad passenger on a cross-country trip realized she was missing her child's special baby formula, a store representative tracked down the formula and met her train during its Chicago layover.

A PORTION OF THE RUG DEPARTMENT
MARSHALL FIELD & CO., RETAIL, CHICAGO

By the 1910s, the store's Oriental rug department was renowned. When the craze for Oriental rugs emerged in the 1880s, Field's responded by sending buyers to Asia. Over the years, the department built a reputation for selling sumptuous antique rugs, as well as custom versions woven to the retailer's specifications. Field's devoted luxurious space to displaying these exotic and often expensive rugs.

Loading delivery wagons. Marshall Field Retail store, Chicago, Ill

Delivery wagons are lined up neatly in this 1897 image of Holden Court, the alley that traversed the store. Initially, boys made deliveries, toting bundles on foot or via public transportation, but in 1873, the firm switched to wagons. By 1907, Marshall Field's used 700 horses and 300 wagons to cover its 350-square-mile delivery area. Stabling and caring for so many horses required a hefty annual budget of $686,000.

Deliveryman Charles Zetek posed with his pristine wagon. The firm prided itself on its elegant wagons and its humane, careful treatment of horses. By 1902, the firm had separate suburban barns at strategic locations around Chicago's outskirts to handle free delivery into the suburbs. Horses remained the dominant mode of delivery well into the early 1900s. (Courtesy Carol Zetek Goddard.)

This custom vehicle from 1911 closely resembles the firm's stylish horse-drawn wagons. The store purchased its first "motor wagons" just after the turn of the century. The earliest delivery cars were electric because, as a store guidebook explained, "the odor of gasoline . . . injures the goods to quite an extent."

Seen here in 1909, the elegant restaurant over the Tiffany dome was originally called the South Grill Room. The bold selection of grilled foods was meant to distinguish the South Grill Room and other "grills" from the daintier tearooms. Still, as these ladies in plumed hats and sweeping skirts show, women quickly adopted both the grills and the tearooms as their own. An early city guidebook explained that Chicago department-store restaurants "are almost invariably crowded, and it is not worth the while of male visitors to try to get meals at them." The restaurants' role was not to make money (they usually operated at a loss) but rather to lure hungry visitors into the store and give those already inside a reason to stay. Their upper-floor location required diners to navigate past enticing impulse goods while making their way upstairs. Because so many customers spoke of this restaurant by referring to its Circassian walnut paneling, it was later renamed the Walnut Grill and then, simply, the Walnut Room. (Courtesy Chicago History Museum, *Chicago Daily News* negatives collection, DN-0007502.)

A building (right), identical in architecture to those on State Street, opened in 1906 on Wabash Avenue, just north of the annex of 1893. Field had earlier bought up stores along this stretch of Wabash Avenue, just as he had on State Street. Clearly, both Field and Shedd intended the store to eventually occupy the entire block.

MARSHALL FIELD & CO.'S RETAIL STORE, CHICAGO

VACCINATION

In co-operation with the Health Department of the city of Chicago, we require that each employe furnish us with a physician's certificate of vaccination, showing proper protection against smallpox.

MANNER OF DRESS

Be cleanly and neat in appearance, avoiding extravagance and display. Women and girls of all Sections, Workrooms, Offices, etc., will be required to wear black skirts at all seasons of the year. No exception can be made to this rule, even to the wearing of large or specially made black aprons over colored skirts. In fact, when any of our women leave their individual sections, they will remove their aprons and scissors. From March 15th to October 15th each year they may wear shirt waists, in white or black (white preferred), white with black stripes or dots, black with white stripes or dots (stripes narrow and dots small), or natural color pongee or linen. From October 15th to March 15th we prefer that they wear black waists but will not object to shirt waists as above. During extremely warm weather, round neck, collarless waists may be worn, the neck to be finished with an edge or insertion. Square or V shape collars must be avoided. Waists of very sheer, unbusinesslike material over colors, or with a great amount of insertion, and black waists with pipings,

plaitings, or bands of color must not be worn. Only full length sleeve waists will be allowed during business hours. Sleeve protectors may be worn by salespeople only during the time that stock work is being done; and this should never be later than 10:30 a. m. Office help and others who do not come in contact with customers may wear sleeve protectors during the day, but will remove them whenever they leave their desks, white protectors will be worn with white waists and black, with black waists.

We prefer a becoming and businesslike arrangement of the hair. Our girls and women will avoid all extreme styles of hair dressing.

Men will avoid unusual color combinations of hosiery and neckwear and loud flashy apparel. When not wearing vests in warm weather they will always keep their coats buttoned.

BULLETIN BOARDS

The bulletin boards in the wash rooms and elsewhere are the official means of communication with employes. Hereon are posted, from time to time, notices which concern every member of the organization. It is therefore highly important that you read each notice as soon as it is posted, and act immediately in accordance with the instructions.

PARCEL PASSES

All packages from outside must be taken to the Pass-Out Desk immediately upon your entering

10

11

The employee rule book from 1911 stipulated businesslike black skirts and long-sleeved shirtwaists (blouses) for women and nothing loud or flashy for men. The rule book also insisted on correct speech ("gentleman" not "gents," for example) and utmost courtesy. Because employee appearance and behavior shaped the firm's overall reputation, supervisors closely monitored employees, requiring that they conform at all times to the firm's atmosphere of genteel respectability.

Opened in 1914, another addition at the corner of Randolph Street and Wabash Avenue finally fulfilled Field and Shedd's dream that the store would occupy an entire city block. This striking image was made by mounting two photographs together to look like one. (Courtesy Historic Architecture and Landscape Image Collection, Ryerson and Burnham Archives, Art Institute of Chicago, digital file No. 16483, © Art Institute of Chicago.)

Opened in 1914, the Narcissus Tea Room took its name from the bronze statue atop its fountain. The room's decor was inspired by Pompeii, including chair designs from a Greek vase and silverware adapted from utensils at the Field Museum. The statue was based on one found in Pompeii, wrongly identified as Narcissus. After closing in 1987, the Narcissus Room became an employee lunchroom and then a special events room.

In 1914, Shedd launched a new store magazine called *Fashions of the Hour*. While clearly promotional, the magazine included literary essays, poetry, and listings of upcoming Chicago events. This issue from December 1916 carried articles about the Art Institute's new east wing and a list of singers in upcoming opera roles alongside gift ideas for Christmas. The soft-sell approach strengthened the store's reputation for putting helpful service ahead of crass commercialism.

Elegant cover illustrations commissioned from prominent artists gave *Fashions of the Hour* chic prestige and set it apart from the mammoth mail-order retail catalogs of Montgomery Ward and others. *Fashions of the Hour* initially came out six times annually, in runs of up to 125,000. Over time, however, the editorial content disappeared, and *Fashions of the Hour* became simply a catalog. In 1979, the name was abandoned.

THE MARSHALL FIELD & CO'S ANNEX BUILDING
WABASH AVE. AND WASHINGTON ST.
CHICAGO

In 1914, a new Field's building (sometimes confusingly called the annex) was constructed at the southwest corner of Washington Street and Wabash Avenue. The Store for Men occupied the first six floors and three basements, with rental tenants above. Shedd claimed he wanted men with their smelly cigars out of the main store, although a separate space undeniably appealed to male shoppers. The original annex building constructed in 1893 is visible at right.

Seen here in the 1950s, the main floor of the Store for Men copied the look and feel of the main store. Note the two-story pillars, open atrium with railings, and round-edged display cases. Still, the masculine merchandise and lack of hordes of female shoppers lured in men who might feel uncomfortable amidst the hosiery and perfume of the main store. By 1915, women made up an estimated 90 percent of all department store customers.

For men who disliked dining in a feminine tearoom, the Store for Men's sixth-floor, 750-seat Men's Grill had the feel of a men's club with bulky walnut furniture, tablecloth-free tables, and a Tiffany-glass dome. The rule barring female diners appealed to businessmen seeking a quick meal or business lunch. The grill had closed by the 1950s, and the space was converted to selling space.

Uniformed men posed with operator Blanche Hildebrand inside one of the store's 76 elevators, probably during World War I. Field's contributed vigorously to the war effort, designing window displays honoring the Allies and opening a third-floor War Service Bureau. A service flag that hung in the south rotunda bore 1,197 stars—one for each Marshall Field employee serving in the military. (Courtesy Chicago History Museum, *Chicago Daily News* negatives collection, DN-0070326.)

A store ban on boyishly short bobbed hair in 1921 caught the attention of the *New York Times*. Having determined that bobbed hair was undignified, the firm ordered all saleswomen with short hair to wear hairnets. As bobbed hair gained popularity and respectability, however, the ban quietly faded away.

Shedd pushed for the firm to increase its manufacturing operations to better compete with other wholesale manufacturers. By the 1920s, the company owned and operated its own mills and factories in North Carolina, Virginia, and Philadelphia. It purchased from others as far away as China. These operations poured out bedspreads, sheets, tablecloths, towels, laces, rugs, knit underwear, hosiery, and other items, all styled and monitored for quality by Marshall Field's.

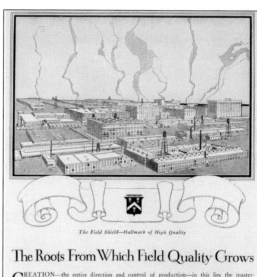

The Field Shield—Hallmark of High Quality

The Roots From Which Field Quality Grows

CREATION—the entire direction and control of production—in this lies the masterstroke of constructive merchandising. Gradually, but with an ever-increasing realization of the need, we have added mill by mill, factory by factory to this organization, until today a panorama of its industries would cover an interesting area of miles. In addition entire outputs of other mills are converted to our uses—delivered in an unfinished state to receive the fine finishing touches which achieve Marshall Field & Company standards.

In the creation of quality in merchandise Marshall Field & Company exercises every facility at its command to insure integrity. Raw materials of the highest standards; processes in spinning and weaving that strengthen and refine; dyeing that stands the severest test of sunlight; our own patterns and designs—these sum up a service that spells quality in merchandise.

The high standards set in our own mills and factories serve as a model for all mills and factories whose output we control. Wherever the influence of Marshall Field & Company operates, there Quality abides.

THE LIST BELOW GIVES ONLY THOSE INDUSTRIES OWNED AND OPERATED BY MARSHALL FIELD & COMPANY

1. Knit Underwear Mill, Leaksville, N. C.
2. Knit Underwear Spinning Mill, Leaksville, N. C.
3. Wearwell Bedspread Mill, Leaksville, N. C.
4. Field Quality Bag Mill, Chicago.
5. Fieldale Spinning and Weaving Mill, Fieldale, Va.
6. Home Crest Mills, Philadelphia, Pa.
7. Fieldale Bleachery, Finishing Mill and Warehouse, Fieldale, Va.
8. American Finishing Mill and Spray Bleachery, Spray, N. C.
9. Warehouses, Chicago.
10. Warehouse, Chicago.
11. Warehouse, Chicago.
12. Bedding Factory, Chicago.
13. Warehouse, Chicago.
14. Warehouse, Chicago.
15. Wearwell Sheeting Mill and Weaving Room of Wearwell Blanket Mill, Draper, N. C.
16. Wholesale Store, Chicago.
17. Nantucket Gingham Mill, Spray, N. C.
18. Rhode Island Blanket Mill, Spray, N. C.
19. Wearwell Blanket Mill, Draper, N. C.
20. Lily Gingham Mill, Spray, N. C.
21. Spray Woolen Mill, Spray, N. C.
22. Tippecanoe Mill, Monticello, Ind.
23. Zion Lace Industries, Zion City, Ill.

By the 1920s, one could walk south from Marshall Field's (far left), and within two blocks encounter Chas. A. Stevens, Mandel Brothers, and Carson, Pirie, Scott (far right). Also nearby were the Boston Store, The Fair, and Siegel, Cooper & Company. Field's work to concentrate Chicago's retail trade around his store had succeeded—maybe too well. Huge crowds were causing some to begin avoiding the jam-packed area altogether.

Marshall Field & Company entered a new era in May 1928 when it opened a branch store in well-heeled Lake Forest, initially carrying just infants' wear and children's wear. Three years later, it moved into a larger building (seen here in the 1960s), which visually echoed the downtown store. It differed from future branches in its limited number of departments and smaller square footage. (Courtesy Chicago History Museum, ICHi-62402.)

By the 1930s, Chicago boasted two lakefront museums that owed much to Marshall Field & Company. At the close of the 1893 World's Columbian Exposition, Marshall Field gave $1 million to endow a museum for the biological and anthropological collections that had been assembled for the exposition. He left the museum another $8 million in his will. The museum changed its name to the Field Museum of Natural History in 1905 to honor its first major benefactor, and in 1921, the museum moved from its original home in the exposition's fine arts building to a new building (center left) on the lakefront. An aquarium with "the greatest variety of sea life under one roof" opened nearby nine years later, thanks to a donation of $2 million from John G. Shedd. The aquarium (center right) featured fanciful bronze starfish on its doors, light fixtures that resembled starfish and octopi, and more than a million gallons of seawater shipped in by railroad from Florida. Shedd passed away in 1926 and was not around to witness the aquarium's grand opening in May 1930.

Field's opened two suburban branches in 1929: one to the west in Oak Park and the other, seen here, to the north in Evanston. The two stores closely resembled each other with bronze corner clocks and French Renaissance architecture by Graham, Anderson, Probst & White (successors to D.H. Burnham & Company). Although smaller than the State Street store, both promised that anything not in stock could be quickly obtained from downtown. (Courtesy Evanston History Center.)

D.E. Frederick, co-founder of Seattle's prestigious and elegant Frederick & Nelson department store (pictured), sold his company to Marshall Field's in 1929 for $6 million. Frederick had patterned many of his firm's policies on Field's, including an emphasis on service and fashionable, high-quality merchandise. With the acquisition came the rights to the firm's trademarked Frango, a name destined to become as beloved in Chicago as it was in Seattle.

Antarctic explorer and pioneer aviator Richard Byrd visited in 1930 to sign copies of his book, *Little America*. Marcella Burns Hahner, the powerful book buyer at Field's, had pioneered the concept of the author signing in 1914. Over the years, the list of authors who came to Field's included Somerset Maugham, Aldous Huxley, Theodore Dreiser, Willa Cather, Carl Sandburg, Gertrude Stein, Shirley Temple, and Amelia Earhart. (Courtesy Richard E. Byrd and Library of Congress, Prints and Photographs Division, LC-USZ62-119039.)

TOYS do for children, what literature and art do for their elders—supply the mind with images and develop breadth and activity of thought

In the great all-the-year-round Toy Section in Marshall Field & Company's store in Chicago

As dime stores and neighborhood toy shops proliferated, Field's positioned itself to fit emerging ideas about the need for stimulating toys in child development. As in most things, Field's did not originate the concept of a year-round toy department (just down the street, discounter Siegel-Cooper opened one in 1908). Field's opened its permanent toy department around 1912, and in doing so, it announced its commitment to sell higher-quality and more developmentally useful merchandise.

The store often showcased theatrical costumes, such as this wedding gown from the 1932 musical *Of Thee I Sing*, in its windows. Note the stylized Art Deco backdrop, typical of Fraser, who loved placing minimal merchandise in elaborate, meticulously authentic settings. Fraser also introduced realistic papier-mâché mannequins in 1913, replacing heavy plaster mannequins who were either headless or had wax heads that tended to melt in the sun. (Courtesy Chicago History Museum/Hedrich-Blessing, HB-01367-A.)

As a young office boy, James Simpson once demanded a raise on his six-dollar-a-week salary. Field snapped, "When I was your age, I got only five dollars a week," to which Simpson replied, "Maybe that's all you were worth, sir." As president from 1923 to 1930, Simpson pushed for a new wholesale center, convinced that wholesale would always be central to the firm's success. (Courtesy Chicago History Museum, *Chicago Daily News* negatives collection, DN-0087078.)

The magnificent Merchandise Mart, then the world's largest building, loomed over the Chicago River in 1930. Built at a cost of more than $30 million, the mart was intended to serve as both Marshall Field & Company's wholesale center and a consolidated center for the entire city's wholesale trade. The 24-story behemoth filled two city blocks and contained 5,500 windows and four million square feet of floor space. But small-town merchants were dying and in the economic tumult of the early 1930s, Field's wholesale division continued to decline. Wholesale posted a staggering $8 million loss in 1932. On the advice of experts, the firm began slashing departments, eventually subjecting the company to what *Fortune* magazine called "one of the bloodiest purges in all merchandising history." By 1936, the entire division was gone. The firm would no longer resell merchandise purchased from manufacturers other than itself. Although Field's still occupied space in the building, in 1945, it sold the money-losing Merchandise Mart to Boston financier and former ambassador Joseph P. Kennedy.

An urbane advertisement from 1930 singles out the sophisticated Field's buyers who select the most up-to-date Continental fashions and "almost anything you might like from Paris." French fashions first made a splash at the World's Columbian Exposition in 1893, after which Field's began importing French designs. As other department stores followed suit, Field's emphasized the authenticity and superior styling of its Parisian originals.

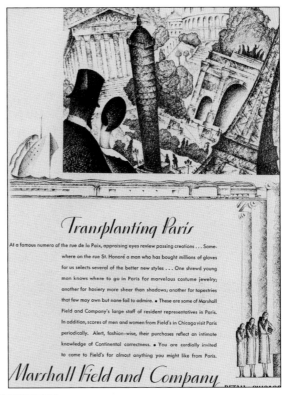

Transplanting Paris

At a famous numero of the rue de la Paix, appraising eyes review passing creations . . . Somewhere on the rue St. Honoré a man who has bought millions of gloves for us selects several of the better new styles . . . One shrewd young man knows where to go in Paris for marvelous costume jewelry; another for hosiery more sheer than shadows; another for tapestries that few may own but none fail to admire. ● These are some of Marshall Field and Company's large staff of resident representatives in Paris. In addition, scores of men and women from Field's in Chicago visit Paris periodically. Alert, fashion-wise, their purchases reflect an intimate knowledge of Continental correctness. ● You are cordially invited to come to Field's for almost anything you might like from Paris.

Marshall Field and Company

. . . Rendezvous

A distinguished educator, looking unusually amiable, is enjoying stuffed lobster in the Mission Grill . . . a well-known actor and his exquisitely dressed companion are discussing the new poetry over coffee in the Walnut Grill at Marshal Field's . . . in the Narcissus Room a charming sophisticate, undeniably Continental, is the center of a laughing group . . . while a tour of the Crystal, Colonial, and Wedgwood Rooms (as well as the Men's Grill in The Store for Men) reveals a significant number of other delightful persons. They may be famous, or just obviously Nice People, but too many of them meet here to call it coincidence. Field's Tea Rooms are an institution in Chicago life; they are the accepted rendezvous for luncheon, tea, or even breakfast among Chicago's better families. You are cordially invited to Field's Tea Rooms when you next visit this city.

Marshall Field and Company

RETAIL CHICAGO

Another advertisement from 1930 clearly reveals the retail store's targeted customer: the "distinguished educator, . . . well-known actor, . . . [and the Continental] sophisticate" . . . in short, anyone wanting to be seen among the "best families." Aimed at out-of-towners, this advertisement appealed to the vanity of anyone who aspired to be one of the "Nice People." The restaurants, and implicitly the store, were part of the process by which Chicago families established and maintained their social status.

Flags from countries around the world billowed across the main aisle for the Century of Progress International Exposition in 1933 and 1934. The immensely popular fair, which attracted more than 48 million visitors to Chicago over its two seasons, included an impressive array of international exhibits, pavilions, and picturesque "villages" to illustrate the technology and achievements of other countries.

Bowing to reports that escalators increased sales by encouraging shoppers to venture above the first floor, Field's paid a hefty $600,000 to install modern, aluminum-sided, double-wide versions in the 1930s. Field's had resisted escalators for decades, both for their rattling noisiness and their association with overcrowded, lower class stores. Westinghouse executives overcame opposition by achieving a design with a sleek, modern style and quiet, smooth ride.

With its celebration of technological innovation, the Century of Progress gave the store an incentive to forge ahead with expensive updates to impress out-of-town visitors. Renovations included refurbishing the silver and jewelry sections with sleek modern light fixtures that set off the mahogany display cases and green marble floors. Here, Field's sold not only modern jewelry and silver tea services, but also custom pieces designed by store artisans and antique silver "with the hallmarks of the best old English silversmiths." The linear, geometric look matched the Art Deco style that was the Century of Progress's trademark. The store also indulged in some new technologies of its own, including partial air conditioning. (Courtesy Chicago History Museum/ Hedrich-Blessing, HB-01809-J.)

Dolls march across the tops of display cases in the toy department in the 1930s. Note the playful wall lettering, oversized robot figure, and other child-friendly displays. Designed to appeal to children separately from adults, these enticing new display strategies had been unknown in 19th-century stores.

A photograph from a store guidebook shows workers making and packing chocolates in the daylight workroom on the store's top floor. At a time when the public frequently distrusted the safety of prepared food, the workers' white hats and coats testified to the store's insistence on cleanliness and purity.

Pillars mark the front door to the Modern House, one of several sample interior-design house displays. Furniture became more important to Marshall Field's in the 20th century than it ever had been in the 1800s. By the 1930s, furniture had become one of the most important departments, with displays that showed various pieces arranged in cozy, coordinated ensembles.

Sleek delivery cars bore the store's crest, an adaptation of the Field family coat of arms. The store delivered merchandise north as far as Waukegan, and south as far as Gary, Indiana. The personal shopping service's motto, "We'll deliver a needle and we'll pick it up," underscored its commitment to service. By the early 1950s, the store had 314 delivery trucks and 52 cars, averaging 25,000 deliveries daily.

Rose Mary, Catherine, and Joan England from Brookfield, Illinois, visited Santa Claus at Marshall Field's in December 1939. "I still remember those reindeer as Field's had them for a number of years," said Joan. "I believe, in looking back, that they were real reindeer that were stuffed by a taxidermist. I know they weren't alive but they appeared to be, except they were stationary." (Courtesy Joan England.)

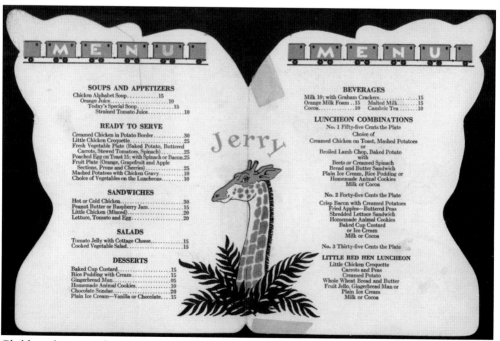

MENU

SOUPS AND APPETIZERS
Chicken Alphabet Soup............15
   Orange Juice........................10
   Today's Special Soup..............15
   Strained Tomato Juice..............10

READY TO SERVE
Creamed Chicken in Potato Border............30
Little Chicken Croquette.......................25
Fresh Vegetable Plate (Baked Potato, Buttered
   Carrots, Stewed Tomatoes, Spinach).........25
Poached Egg on Toast 15; with Spinach or Bacon.25
Fruit Plate (Orange, Grapefruit and Apple
   Sections, Prune and Cherries)................25
Mashed Potatoes with Chicken Gravy..............10
Choice of Vegetables on the Luncheons.........10

SANDWICHES
Hot or Cold Chicken.........................30
Peanut Butter or Raspberry Jam..............15
Little Chicken (Minced)......................20
Lettuce, Tomato and Egg......................20

SALADS
Tomato Jelly with Cottage Cheese.............15
Cooked Vegetable Salad.......................15

DESSERTS
Baked Cup Custard.....................15
Rice Pudding with Cream...............15
Gingerbread Man.......................05
Homemade Animal Cookies...............10
Chocolate Sundae......................20
Plain Ice Cream—Vanilla or Chocolate....15

Jerry

MENU

BEVERAGES
Milk 10; with Graham Crackers.............15
Orange Milk Foam ..15   Malted Milk........15
Cocoa...............10   Cambric Tea 10

LUNCHEON COMBINATIONS
No. 1 Fifty-five Cents the Plate
Choice of
Creamed Chicken on Toast, Mashed Potatoes
or
Broiled Lamb Chop, Baked Potato
with
Beets or Creamed Spinach
Bread and Butter Sandwich
Plain Ice Cream, Rice Pudding or
Homemade Animal Cookies
Milk or Cocoa

No. 2 Forty-five Cents the Plate
Crisp Bacon with Creamed Potatoes
Fried Apples—Buttered Peas
Shredded Lettuce Sandwich
Homemade Animal Cookies
Baked Cup Custard
or Ice Cream
Milk or Cocoa

No. 3 Thirty-five Cents the Plate

LITTLE RED HEN LUNCHEON
Little Chicken Croquette
Carrots and Peas
Creamed Potato
Whole Wheat Bread and Butter
Fruit Jello, Gingerbread Man or
Plain Ice Cream
Milk or Cocoa

Children dining in the store's restaurants in the 1930s got their own menu. Like most department stores, Field's made modest efforts to appeal to children's tastes by offering milk and special desserts, but for the most part, the child-friendly meals were variations on the standard adult fare, with meat, vegetables, and potatoes dominating the suggested combinations.

Shown posing alongside a china cupboard, first lady Eleanor Roosevelt visited in 1939. The store's long list of other famous visitors over the years included Winston Churchill, Bette Davis, Isadora Duncan, Gypsy Rose Lee, Mary Todd Lincoln, Richard Nixon, Theodore Roosevelt, and William Howard Taft. In 1896, Ida McKinley ordered her blue-grey satin inaugural gown from Marshall Field & Company. Mobster Al Capone once purchased 10 silk shirts for $35 each.

Before plastic credit cards arrived in the 1960s, the store issued Charga-Plates to its charge account customers. Each dog-tag-size plate held a paper card with the shopper's signature. The address embossed on the back of the plate could be inked and pressed onto a charge slip. Note the perimeter notches made to fit Marshall Field's Charga-Plate machines, preventing its use at unauthorized stores. The plastic card (rear) is from the 1990s.

A treasured tradition ☆ Gifts from Field's, whether modest or magnificent, are as symbolic of the season as reindeer and holly ☆ A few grand gestures from the Store of the Christmas Spirit ☆ Luxurious sable dyed Russian Kolinsky jacket, the small collar to be caught up with a jewel or turned away from the throat, $595 ☆ 1. Fine Hraba bag in gold and black brocade, lined in gold kid, fittings of black enamel and gold, $105 ☆ 2. By Paul Storr, master silversmith, this gracious Georgian centerpiece, London, 1802. From our famous antique silver collection, $595 ☆ 3. For a pretty wrist, Georgian bracelets in flexible yellow gold, clasped by coral cameos, $300 the pair. A beautiful old English brooch, cabochon garnets and rose diamonds, mounted in gold, $215. Heirloom pieces, all three ☆

Marshall Field & Company
CHICAGO

Marshall Field's gift suggestions for Christmas 1940 in *Vogue* magazine included a sable fur jacket for $595 ($9,000 in today's money), a Georgian silver centerpiece, and an old English brooch. By regularly advertising in national fashion magazines, Field's communicated its position as a leader in fashion and purveyor of high-end luxury goods. Despite wartime shortages, the store enjoyed strong sales in the early 1940s.

Rows of manicure tables in the fifth-floor beauty salon testify to the popularity of the salon, which offered facials, body treatments, hairstyling, makeup, waves, pedicures, and other chic pampering treatments. Like restaurants and waiting rooms, the beauty salon encouraged shoppers to see the store as a clubhouse or social center. As a place of constant, ever-changing amusement, Marshall Field's became a destination for daylong outings. (Courtesy Chicago History Museum/Hedrich-Blessing, HB-05194-B.)

C-167

Sleek, elegant, and classically spare, the oval-shaped 28 Shop on the sixth floor opened in 1941 as the place to shop for haute couture in Chicago and "the fashion center of mid-America." Although physically within the store, the exclusive sixth-floor shop had a separate exterior entrance and its own posh elevator. Its name came from its entrance at 28 East Washington Street. Joseph Platt, set designer for *Gone With the Wind* in 1939, designed the department around a circular salon. The fitting rooms, 28 in all, circled the main salon. They were lavishly appointed and decorated in pairs. Two were adorned in black and peach, two were paneled in bamboo, two were mirrored, two were finished in pigskin, and so on. By 1944, sales at the 28 Shop reached $1.2 million. As soon as World War II ended and French imports were available again, Field's buyers attended overseas couture openings, reportedly sending back more European designs than any other American store. Some were sold, while others were copied and reworked into American versions. "A few weeks after Balenciaga introduces a new jacket line," a store guidebook said, "you'll find it at Field's, adapted for every figure type, every age, every purse."

American designer Adrian's full-skirted gown shows the impact of Christian Dior's New Look. Adrian (Adrian Adolph Greenberg), a costume designer for Metro-Goldwyn-Mayer in the 1930s and 1940s, had opened an independent fashion house that sold to only one store in each major city. Such exclusivity appealed to Field's. The firm had been negotiating sole rights since 1880, when it acquired exclusive rights to sell the famous Alexandre kid gloves in America.

An array of sports clothes in this window display hints at the more informal lifestyle increasingly adopted by women. Introduced in the 1890s as clothing for specific sports such as golf, bicycling, skiing, or tennis, sportswear took off as everyday wear. The casual cuts and informal fabrics suited Americans' increasingly informal lifestyles. By the 1950s, sportswear would be the biggest category of women's clothing.

The second-floor wedding bureau prospered during and after World War II. The bureau helped brides with everything from choosing gifts for attendants and solving sticky etiquette issues to furnishing a new home. During the war, the store linked wedding traditions to American patriotism with window displays showing wartime brides marrying uniformed soldiers, as a reminder of what the soldiers were fighting to defend. (Courtesy Chicago History Museum/Hedrich-Blessing, HB-06375.)

A window decorated for Christmas 1941 drips with gift suggestions: elegant dress shoes, embroidered and lace collars, gloves, and beaded boleros. Prior to World War II, the store's December window displays typically featured gift ideas and holiday-themed tableaux. The first narrative story windows appeared in 1944, the year Arthur Fraser retired. That year, the windows sequentially narrated Clement C. Moore's poem "A Visit from St. Nicholas."

A barrage balloon, usually used during World War II to deter low-flying enemy aircraft, hung strategically in the north light well as an eye-catching reminder to shoppers to visit the Victory Center upstairs. The store regularly drummed up patriotism and support for the war by displaying donated examples of equipment and machinery being used in the war effort. (Courtesy Chicago History Museum/Hedrich-Blessing, HB-07538.)

The ninth-floor Victory Center displayed photographs and maps that showed recent troop activities, posted the latest news bulletins, and sold defense bonds and stamps. It also provided meeting space for war relief and fundraising organizations. (Courtesy Chicago History Museum/Hedrich-Blessing, HB-06852-B.)

Unlike other department stores such as The Fair, Marshall Field & Company never sold staple groceries. In 1943, however, it opened a gourmet food department called the Pantry. This advertisement from the back of a Field's menu emphasizes the healthfulness, quality, and purity of its foods. In 1947, the company began delivering frozen meals to customers who had freezers.

Field's helped drum up support for World War II in a series of window displays, such as this one urging viewers to save tin. The store worked hard to stir up positive feelings for the war effort and link everyday household goods to war production. Other windows urged Chicagoans to buy Liberty Bonds, save food and rubber, and contribute to the Red Cross. (Courtesy Chicago History Museum/ Hedrich-Blessing, HB-07101-A.)

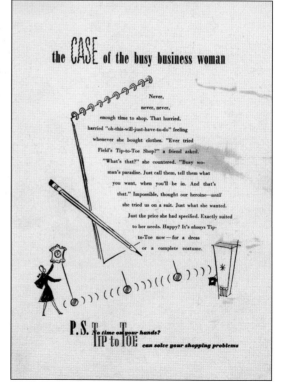

The back of an English Room menu from 1945 reminded busy shoppers to use the Tip-To-Toe Shop, where clerks could put together an entire wardrobe. Allegedly, a hurried Australian pilot once stopped by with a snapshot of his wife and a few details of her social life. When he returned a few hours later, the store had assembled for him a full wardrobe suitable for her figure—and his wallet.

When one Chicago matron heard about the Japanese attack on Pearl Harbor in 1941, she reportedly declared, "Nothing is left any more—except, thank God, Marshall Field's." After the announcement of Japan's surrender four years later in August 1945, Field's celebrated the Allied victory by hanging American flags from nearly every State Street window. In the center, an enormous eight-story V proclaimed victory.

The book section bustled with activity during the holiday season of 1946. Acclaimed as "the largest [book seller] in this hemisphere," Marshall Field's book section sold more best sellers than any other store; it also offered valuable first editions and collector's volumes. Yet when Selfridge had first suggested a book department, Field grumbled, "Let Colonel McClurg [owner of a nearby bookstore] sell the books. We're in the dry-goods business."

71

Norman Rockwell immortalized the store's clocks on the cover of the *Saturday Evening Post* magazine from November 3, 1945. Rockwell's sentimental illustration helped cement the store's status as an American icon, although the clocks were actually set from inside the store. Rockwell donated the painting to the store in 1948. (Courtesy Norman Rockwell Family Agency, © 1945 The Norman Rockwell Family Entities.)

Four

POSTWAR BOOM AND SUBURBAN EXPANSION

(1946–1981)

In 1946, the store debuted a chubby, red-coated, gauzy-winged character named Uncle Mistletoe. Created by Johanna Osborne at the request of John Moss in the display department, Uncle Mistletoe got his look from Osborne's husband Addis, an art instructor who drew the original sketches of a Dickensian character with bushy eyebrows and a top hat. Uncle Mistletoe first appeared in a Christmas window narrative that had him helping two children visit the North Pole.

"Uncle Mistletoe in Wonderland"

with Uncle Mistletoe and Aunt Judy
and Tony Pony, Obediah Pig
and Michael O'Hare

*copyright 1949, Marshall Field & Company

Marshall Field & Company

Chicago

Uncle Mistletoe—and his spouse Aunt Holly, introduced in 1948—spun off into other mediums, including a record album and television show. Popular children's actor Johnny Coon voiced Uncle Mistletoe, spreading word of his Kindness Club. To join, children had to submit a letter describing one good deed they had performed. Uncle Mistletoe's popularity soon rivaled that of Howdy Doody. *Billboard* magazine declared him "hotter than Mr. Claus." (Courtesy Carol Zetek Goddard.)

Merry Christmas
Uncle Mistletoe and
Aunt Holly

During the 1950s and 1960s, Uncle Mistletoe and Aunt Holly grew so wildly popular that the store hired actors to portray them for children visiting Santa Claus. To pass the time as children waited for up to two hours outside Santa's Cozy Cloud Cottage on the eighth floor, Uncle Mistletoe and Aunt Holly greeted visitors and handed out official Kindness Club buttons.

The 1948 holiday catalog carried two items destined to become coveted collectibles. Uncle Mistletoe appears as an doll for $8.95, one of hundreds of Uncle Mistletoe merchandise items that eventually included ornaments, greeting cards, barware, coloring books, carved candles, mugs, and figural cookie jars. The toy semi truck, available here for $8.95, was a private-label item available only at Marshall Field & Company stores and therefore manufactured in smaller quantities than other toy trucks.

The Assembly Room handled clothing for preteens and teenagers in sizes 10 to 16. While located on the fourth floor with other children's merchandise, the department recognized the separate needs of preteen and young teenage girls who wanted clothing distinct from that offered for younger children. Department stores were in the vanguard of nurturing young women's evolution as consumers. (Courtesy Chicago History Museum/ Hedrich-Blessing, HB-10553-A.)

Time-crunched shoppers could head for the second floor's Gift Court, which showcased gift-worthy merchandise from throughout the store: games, handkerchiefs, candies, books, perfumes, pipes, lamps, and so on. Tourists were key shoppers here. A New York businessman reportedly once broke up a conference so he could shop before flying home. "My youngsters would never forgive me if I came home without a present from Field's," he explained.

A long line at the customer service desk just after Christmas 1946 speaks to Marshall Field's ongoing reputation for graciously taking back merchandise. The company's huge size reduced its costs of business and made it easier to absorb the cost of returned goods. Because its reputation for taking back almost anything helped business, Field's kept its liberal returns policy.

Neatly lined up at their stations with their starter (left), the store's uniformed elevator girls grew so famous that *Life* magazine ran a feature article in 1947 about their eight-week charm school and beauty course. The twice-weekly program included hair and makeup lessons as well as training on how to walk, sit, and operate the elevator cars "decorously." Most elevator operators probably yearned to follow Mary Leta Lambour, better known as Dorothy Lamour. After winning a New Orleans beauty contest in 1931, Lambour moved to Chicago and worked briefly as a $17-a-week Marshall Field's elevator girl before becoming a cabaret singer and then movie star. Other Field's employees who became celebrities include first lady Nancy Davis Reagan (sales clerk), catalog sales pioneer Aaron Montgomery Ward (sales clerk and traveling salesman), and film and stage director Vincent Minnelli (window decorator). (Courtesy George Skadding/Time Life Pictures/ Getty Images.)

The *Chicago Sun-Times* dubbed Helen Sarros "queen of the mighty basement console" in a photograph from 1947 publicizing the store's new pneumatic system. First installed in 1893, pneumatic vacuum tubes initially replaced "cash boys" in transporting customers' money to the cashiering department. Later, after cash registers took over, the tubes carried notes between stockrooms and sales floors, sent refund tickets to be cashed, and performed other messenger tasks. (Courtesy *Chicago Sun-Times*.)

A labyrinth of chutes and conveyer belts carried packages to the first sub-basement where workers weighed, sorted, and rerouted them according to destination. In the 1940s, the store delivered as many as 95,000 packages each day. Still further underground, in the third sub-basement, sat the power center where long trains of cars came in through the freight tunnels with coal for the store's furnaces and went out carrying heaps of rubbish.

Advertisements for Marshall Field's chocolate mint Frango candies first appeared around 1947, although they had been developed at Frederick & Nelson in 1927. Popular legend held that the candies were originally called "Franco" mints but were renamed in the 1930s to avoid association with Spain's fascist dictator Francisco Franco. However, US patent office documents show that Frederick & Nelson trademarked "Frango" in 1918—long before Franco rose to power.

By 1947, tea at Field's was a beloved Chicago tradition. Plumed hats, curled hair, and best clothes came out, as did best manners. The store then had five grills and tearooms and served about 7,000 diners daily, not including the basement fountain dinette. The tradition lingered—although increasingly just as a Christmas tradition—into the 21st century. (Courtesy Chicago History Museum/M. J. Schmidt, ICHi-38786.)

Rows of sleek modern kitchen ranges and refrigerators speak to shoppers' enthusiasm for technology after World War II. Department stores played a major role in demonstrating the benefits of modern appliances, both in function and in looks. For Chicagoans looking to update their homes, modern appliances often claimed first priority. (Courtesy Chicago History Museum/Hedrich-Blessing, HB-11306-T.)

Certain items from the Marshall Field's bakery, such as fruitcake, became celebrities. Introduced in 1948, a nut-studded molasses treat called the hermit cookie featured mocha frosting and a recipe that changed little in the 40-odd years it was offered. The store had more than 5,000 recipes for foods sold in the restaurants and food departments, some of them kept locked in the corporate safe. (Courtesy Chicago History Museum/Hedrich-Blessing, HB-11306-W.)

Inexpensive notions such as thread, thimbles, and needles still held a prominent position on the main floor in 1947. Even though fewer and fewer women sewed their own clothes by the middle of the 20th century, notions remained on the ground floor long after fabrics and patterns had been banished to upper floors. (Courtesy Chicago History Museum/Hedrich-Blessing, HB-11306-B.)

Over time, the notions section expanded to encompass not only ribbons but also hair ornaments, closet accessories, and sunglasses. A study done in 1967 showed that half of downtown department store shoppers made a purchase in the notions department—and 84 percent of them visited other departments. (Courtesy Chicago History Museum/Hedrich-Blessing, HB-11306-H.)

By the time this advertisement from 1948 appeared, twinsets of closely fitting pullovers and matching cardigans were hitting the zenith of their popularity. Fueled by fashion icons such as Audrey Hepburn and Grace Kelly, they became de rigueur for college girls and many others in the 1950s. Marshall Field's advertised this version in hand-knit cashmere with a subtle hint at the attention it would draw.

Chicago's Municipal Airport (later known as Midway) opened a new terminal in 1948 that featured an elegant 24-hour restaurant run by Marshall Field's. The Cloud Room offered dramatic floor-to-ceiling views of the tarmac and delicacies such as pineapple flown in from Hawaii. Field's also ran the airport's informal Blue and Gold Café—allegedly a favorite of Frank Sinatra. Midway's supremacy receded after O'Hare Airport opened, and the Cloud Room closed in 1962.

The English Room, which overlooked the magnificent north light well, served from this menu on July 17, 1950. Diners that day could have enjoyed two famous Field's dishes: corned beef hash and the sandwich known as the Special, which consisted of a lettuce wedge, chicken, Swiss cheese, and bacon served open-faced on rye bread and smothered in Thousand Island dressing. The "maple Frango" is probably the mousse-like dessert originated by Frederick & Nelson.

Marshall Field & Company president James Palmer (far left) joined shopping center developer Philip M. Klutznick (in glasses, holding pick) and other officials to break ground in 1949 for a new shopping center in suburban Park Forest. One of the first shopping centers in the nation, Park Forest Plaza boasted a three-story, 116,000-square-foot Marshall Field's store, dedicated in 1955. It closed in 1996. (Courtesy Park Forest Historical Society.)

Field's Famous Foods

3—Oven browned corned beef hash made from freshly cooked corned beef, and served in a casserole, special dressing, tossed vegetable salad with garlic croutons, oil and vinegar dressing 1.00

4—Special sandwich: sliced breast of chicken, Swiss cheese, tomato and hard cooked egg on rye bread, Thousand Island dressing, crisp bacon, ripe olive, served with coffee 1.25

Cream of corn and pimiento soup 20-40   Tomato broth with rice 15-30

Luncheon Suggestions

40—Breaded lamb cutlet, mint jelly, parsley new potatoes, carrots with peas . . 1.00
41—From the grill: (allow 20 minutes for broiling)
Filet of bluefish, lemon wedge, parsley new potatoes, Harvard beets . 1.15
42—Hot flaked chicken sandwich with fricassee gravy, homemade watermelon pickles 90
46—Cold plate: assorted meats, Field's potato salad in a crisp lettuce cup, tomato and cucumber slices 90
47—Italian spaghetti with meat sauce, tossed vegetable salad with garlic croutons, oil and vinegar dressing 65
Choice of honey bran muffin, Melba toast, hard or soft roll
LUNCHEON ACCOMPANIMENT: tossed vegetable salad with garlic croutons, oil and vinegar dressing 20

Desserts

Try creamy rich ice creams and flaky pastries made by experts in our own kitchens

Chilled watermelon 40   Peppermint candy ice cream with cold fudge 25
Field's covered apple pie with cheese 20   Pineapple meringue pie 25
Cherry upside down cake, whipped cream 25   Field's deep dish apple pie 22
Field's maple frango 30   Swiss Gruyere cheese served with salted crackers 35
Strawberry Bavarian cream 20   Chilled peach slices 20
Ice creams: vanilla, chocolate, coffee, maplenut, peach, banana, Burgundy cherry, peppermint stick candy, ginger bisque, chocolate chip, strawberry or lemon custard 20
Sundaes: pineapple, cold fudge or caramel 25; with whipped cream or nuts 30
Sherbets: lemon or cherry 20

An amount will be added to quoted prices of all our food to cover additional expense due to the Illinois Retailers Occupational Tax

An elegantly staged photograph shows doorman Charlie Pritzlaff, a store fixture for more than 50 years, at the Washington Street entrance. Beloved for his friendliness and courtesy, Pritzlaff familiarized himself with the store's most prominent customers by checking customers' names against the society Blue Book. In a nod to his fame and popularity, former employee Emily Kimbrough titled her 1952 store memoir *Through Charley's Door.* (Courtesy Kate Wells.)

By the 1950s, luxury sheets sold under the Fieldcrest label were one of the few remaining signs of the firm's formerly vast manufacturing operations, which had once included 30 mills. The mills initially sold their output to the wholesale division and after wholesale disappeared, to the firm's manufacturing division. With the sale of Fieldcrest Mills in 1953, Marshall Field & Company completed the sell-off of its mill operations as its attention focused on suburban expansion.

Models prepared behind the scenes for fashion shows that took place several times weekly in the 1940s and 1950s. Fashion shows emphasized both high fashion and trends, translating them for any budget or size. "Marshall Field's had more in-store fashion shows than any other department store," reported model Kate Wells (shown above with pearl necklace). "Customers would tell us, 'I feel like I know you.' " (Courtesy Chicago History Museum/ Wesley Bowman, ICHi-61864.)

Kate Wells (right) launched her 12-year career as a Field's model after hearing the store needed a blonde. She dyed her hair with peroxide, took her own photograph in a Woolworth's self-operated booth, and got the job. As the store's public face, models were cautioned to avoid scandal. "We were also expected to dress well, even while out in public on non-working days," she said. (Courtesy Kate Wells.)

Marshall Field's, at left, declared "the Clock Strikes a Century" as it kicked off its 100th anniversary in 1952. Interestingly, for decades the firm had considered its origin to be 1865, and no 50th anniversary had been held in 1902. Setting (or re-setting) the origin date as far back as possible, made Marshall Field's the city's oldest, most established store—only 15 years younger than Chicago itself.

Chairman of the board Hughston McBain toasted guests at the centennial celebration on January 10, 1952. Models wearing dresses representing various decades encircled an artificial 22-foot-high birthday cake as a nostalgic nod to the olden days and a reminder of the store's ongoing fashion prowess. The cake stood in the Walnut Room most of the year, coming down only for Easter and Christmas. Note the extra candle on top "to grow on."

As part of the anniversary, Field's commissioned journalist-authors Lloyd Wendt and Herman Kogan to write a history of the store. *Give the Lady What She Wants* intertwines the history of Marshall Field's with that of Chicago using colorful stories and abundant images from the store archives. The wildly popular book also gave readers a peek at plans for the upcoming Old Orchard shopping center, which was set to open in 1956.

Give the Lady What She Wants!

by Lloyd Wendt and Herman Kogan

...the story of Marshall Field & Company

$4.50

You'll love it as much as we do . . . this vivid, zestful story of one American business. It's a human, humorous history of how we grew, changing along with the changing customs and fashions. But it's not only the story of a store, it's the story of womankind . . . how her housekeeping habits have changed in a century of living and how she put her best foot forward into man's business world — and kept it there! Authors Wendt and Kogan, specialists in the area of colorful characters, revive some of the most interesting folks you've ever met . . . Marshall Field, the aloof perfectionist; Harry Selfridge who staged his own wedding in Central Music Hall; Millie, the shoplifter who, like the society ladies, preferred Field's quality. The book will appear May 5, but to be certain of receiving your copy, reserve one by ordering now. E 324 . . . $4.50. Books—Third Floor

USE THIS HANDY MAP TO HELP YOU FIND YOUR WAY AROUND FIELD'S

NINTH FLOOR

EIGHTH FLOOR — H — G

SEVENTH FLOOR — N

SIXTH FLOOR — D C A

FIFTH FLOOR — B

FOURTH FLOOR — E F

THIRD FLOOR — L

SECOND FLOOR — J K

FIRST FLOOR

WABASH AVE. NORTH WABASH MIDDLE WABASH SOUTH WABASH WASHINGTON

RANDOLPH ST. NORTH STATE MIDDLE STATE SOUTH STATE STATE ST.

SUB-ST. FLOOR — M

Each of Field's ten selling floors is divided into six rooms: North, Middle and South STATE on one side; North, Middle and South WABASH on the other. Listed below you'll find the shops described in this book, along with their specific locations. The letter before each is keyed to a shaded area on the map. Space does not permit us to include the many outstanding departments in Field's. For example, on the ninth floor you'll find a wonderful music center with pianos, television sets, radios and recordings . . . housewares, draperies and decorator fabrics. On the eighth floor, model apartments . . . two acres of furniture, every period, every price. The seventh floor is famous for its five gigantic tea rooms. The sixth floor is devoted to women's fashions, from casual to after-five. You'll find a beauty salon, lingerie, millinery, shoes and accessories on the fifth floor. The fourth is the young people's floor, with everything from infants' wear to fashions for teens. On the third are books of every variety, rugs and candies. The second floor is known for its linen collections, its Gift Court, its fine glassware and china. Use this map as a guide to the shops shown. Then, explore Field's yourself —you'll find many exciting places in Field's that a book this size could never cover.

A 28 Shop®—Sixth Floor, South, Wabash
B Shoe Salon—Fifth Floor, North, State
C Tip to Toe Shop—Sixth Floor, North, State
D Brides' Room—Sixth Floor, North, Wabash
E Assembly Room—Fourth Floor, North, State
F Toy Center—Fourth Floor, Middle, Wabash
G Interior Decorating Galleries—Eighth Floor, North, State
H Trend House—Eighth Floor, North, Wabash
I Georgian Room—First Floor, South, Wabash
J Collectors' Room—Second Floor, South, Wabash
K Gift Court—Second Floor, Middle, State
L Books—Third Floor, North, Wabash
M Budget Floor—Downstairs
N Walnut Room—Seventh Floor, South, State

A simplified directory from 1951 indicates the store's vast size. By this time, some locations were burned into shoppers' minds: children's merchandise on the fourth floor, books on the third, restaurants on the seventh, and interior decorating on the eighth. The Georgian Room on the first floor and Collector's Room on the second housed art and historic items, including antique silver and treasures of famous collectors.

Two German shepherds press a pedal to check in at a watchman's bell station. Although they lasted only a short time, the store's security watchdogs—three at the main store and four in one of the warehouses—caught the attention of *Life* magazine, which ran a brief story on them in March 1952. The dogs proved disconcertingly efficient at cornering employees doing after-hours work. (Courtesy Francis Miller/Time Life Pictures/Getty Images.)

Carpenters and painters worked under the roof amidst disembodied mannequin legs and arms. The move to self-service—spurred by the shortage of clerks during World War II—accelerated the need for talented display artists, as merchandise no longer hid in stockroom-like cabinets. Clear, attractive presentation was now as critical for interior displays as it was for the exterior display windows and first-floor decorations.

In 1953, Cozy Cloud Cottage contained a red chair for Santa Claus with a telescope and a window view of the pastel Aurora Borealis beyond. The oversized book nearby listed names of good girls and boys. Because Cozy Cloud Cottage was the Trend House during the rest of the year, visitors waited in lines that snaked through two or three decorated rooms. (Courtesy Mary Robinson Kalista; from the collection of Lucile Ward Robinson.)

At Christmas, enormous candy canes encircling each pillar transformed the fourth-floor toy department's main aisle into "Candy Cane Lane." Themed scenes around the pillars changed annually. For the festival of lights theme in 1955 seen here, each pillar showed an angel illuminating a different form of Christmas lights. (Courtesy Mary Robinson Kalista; from the collection of Lucile Ward Robinson.)

After the mauve bridal gown appeared in this publicity photograph, a customer purchased it for her own wedding. During the postwar bridal boom, Field's positioned itself as a leading purveyor of bridal traditions, holding regular bridal events such as Bride's Week in 1958, which featured window displays depicting bridal traditions. Brides often formed a lifelong loyalty to the store at the time of their weddings. (Courtesy Chicago History Museum, ICHi-24398.)

Custom-made furs were some of the most celebrated manufactured items made for customers in the store's upper-floor workshops. The store prided itself not only on the furs it made and sold, but also on its vast fur storage vaults. In the summer months of the 1940s, Field's housed some $12 million worth of customer-owned furs in the vaults, which were kept at near-freezing temperatures.

Hunters aim for clay birds at the 192-acre Marshall Field's practice range, Fieldale Farms, which was located in Hoffman Estates. Opened in 1952, the range let would-be hunters practice on artificial ducks, quail, pheasant, and partridge; the cost was $3 for 25 targets. Although it took 10 years of planning and required 40 employees to operate, the range only lasted seven years. Hilldale Golf Club was later built on the grounds. (Courtesy Hoffman Estates Museum.)

As many as 1,400 craftspeople worked for the store. Skilled gunsmiths could repair and remodel any gun, from a sturdy hunting rifle to a custom, gold-plated showpiece. The upper-floor workshops also included a candy kitchen, photographic laboratory, and workshops for stationery, picture framing, jewelry, silver, draperies, shoe repair, custom saddlery, and watch repair. The millinery workroom produced some 20,000 hats annually. (Courtesy Chicago History Museum/Hedrich-Blessing, HB-09478-I.)

By the 1950s, self-service racks and open shelving had largely replaced closed drawers and cabinets. While comfortable chairs still created the expectation of service, merchandise now hung on racks, accessible both visually and physically. (Courtesy Chicago History Museum/ Hedrich-Blessing, HB-20184-B.)

Children colored and played in the store's well-equipped playroom, humorously described as a place where children could be "parked" while their mothers shopped. Besides the playroom, Field's had other features designed to compete for children's—and their parents'—attention: the Jolly Barber Shop, a marionette theater, special music and dance performances, and holiday parties. (Courtesy Wallace Kirkland/Time Life Pictures, Getty Images.)

Influential French fashion designer Christian Dior raised a cup to the fashionability of Chicago women at a press conference held in the 28 Shop in April 1957. Dior complimented Chicago women, saying, "They dress like American women, and that's good." Field's sponsored the French designer's visit to the United States, timed to celebrate the 10th anniversary of the introduction of his full-skirted, round-shouldered "New Look," the fashion trend that launched his leadership in the world of couture fashion. In the 1950s, Dior accounted for half of France's haute couture exports, and he had a close relationship with Marshall Field's, which held exclusive rights to sell Dior in Chicago. With Dior's permission, the store also copied some of his fashions into lower-price "knock-off" versions.

The Walnut Room Christmas tree tradition began in 1907. During the years a fresh tree was used, it would be carried in through the Randolph Street entrance (for which employees temporarily removed the revolving doors) and hoisted up through the north light well to the seventh floor. In the Walnut Room, workers stood ready with block-and-tackle to heave the tree into position atop the drained fountain.

Seeking the world's largest indoor tree, workers annually scoured woods in Minnesota or Michigan for a symmetrical tree about 70 feet tall. The ideal tree's top 50 feet would be shipped by railroad to Chicago for the Walnut Room, as seen here in 1959. Until the store switched to an artificial tree in the early 1960s, a firefighter stood watch 24 hours a day. (Courtesy Chicago History Museum/Clarence W. Hines, ICHi-17139.)

In December 1962, the Marshall Field & Company Choral Society presented its 36th performance of Handel's *Messiah* in the Walnut Room. The society began in 1907, consisted of about 200 employees, and became "a creditable force in Chicago musical life." The group rehearsed on Tuesday evenings and gave concerts in May at Orchestra Hall and at Christmas in the Walnut Room.

Opened in 1962, the Field's store in posh Oakbrook Center was surrounded by flowers and fountains. The new shopping center was close to major expressways and the upscale, young village of Oak Brook, promising a high-end clientele. By 1976, Oakbrook Center was generating more sales tax revenue per square foot of selling space than any other shopping center in the country.

DECORATOR'S DREAM HOUSE

(convenient to escalator)

Now being shown. Luxurious home, including lanai, fountained terrace, weathervane, and landscaping, nestled on spacious eighth floor. The view is all inside.

This is Trend House where new ideas are constantly being born. To express its current theme, which is entertaining in the gracious manner, our staff of decorators, designers, artists, and craftsmen have sketched, planned, and shopped for more than half a year. Superb antiques have been combined with cabinet-made reproductions and the pure inventiveness of our own distinguished designers.

For example, you will see the newest way to do a dining room—with two areas of focus. The formal setting, an enchantment of crystal, gilt, and chalk pink silk; and the informal area with its comfortable banquettes and unexpected black tile floor, inset with coins from Monaco. You may very likely purchase the pair of spectacular, 6 ft. 3-tiered étagères, so typical of the lavish Swiss buffet, and which our decorators created and had made. Ideas run all through Trend House. It was felt the grand piano in the living room needed "something." So our artists executed a delicate, French flower basket motif on the music rack. The walls of this room are covered with a hand-printed fabric tirelessly searched for in Venice. The rug was handmade abroad to our own design. You will undoubtedly notice the English Sheraton period cylinder desk, circa 1790. It is an extremely rare and fine antique and in mint-condition. The 3-phased library includes special lighting effects, an example of how we custom-bind books, how we construct an entire wall to hold a pewter collection, and a new way to hang an Oriental mural. The elegant bedroom-sitting room has its own surprises.

Next time you're in Chicago, come to Field's and see our ever-changing Trend House. It will give you a glimpse of how we can do or re-do an entire home, apartment, or room with imagination and taste. We invite you to use one of the largest and most talented staffs in the country. Interior Decorating, Decorating Galleries, Eighth Floor. There's nothing like it back home.

Marshall Field & Company

Illustrated in this 1963 advertisement and situated on the eighth floor, the Trend House was a model house featuring a full house's worth of decorating ideas. The decor changed regularly to reflect different trends, demonstrate distinctive lighting effects, and display the handiwork of store craftsmen in everything from rug design to bookbinding.

In keeping with Marshall Field's tradition of offering dependably fashionable merchandise, clothing in a 1964 Marshall Field's catalog included embroidered, beaded, and ruffled knits in lamb's wool and angora. The clothing reflected increasingly casual styles, and fabrics now featured acrylic and nylon as often as wool and silk.

An exterior scrubbing brought the store's granite back to its gleaming whiteness but did little to halt shoppers' changing habits in the early 1960s. Lifestyle changes spurred by the automobile and the suburbs were impacting downtown retail. Delivery service declined as more and more customers carried packages home themselves in their cars. Many shoppers preferred shopping at malls thanks to their convenient locations and expansive parking lots. (Courtesy Chicago History Museum/Hedrich-Blessing, HB-24321-C.)

In the 1960s, Field's hired summertime college representatives to promote sales to college students. Wearing designer outfits, coeds from a variety of colleges assisted teenagers in choosing suitable clothing. "Every two weeks we had fashion shows in the famous Walnut Room, wearing everything from PJs to formal dresses. They also gave us lessons on modeling, walking, standing, sitting, plus hair and makeup lessons," said Marilyn Vojta, a representative in 1965.

By the late 1960s, the store's famed toy department still held a cherished place in shoppers' memory, but the discount toy chains and big-box stores (that is, large, freestanding, one-level stores) of the 1970s took a big bite out of department store sales. (Courtesy Chicago History Museum/Hedrich-Blessing, HB-32286-b.)

Field's record department sold a huge range of merchandise. Former staffer Susan Greene recalled, "Apart from phonograph records and 45s, we sold ukuleles, guitars, bongo drums, harmonicas, kazoos, recorders, tambourines, castanets, metronomes, music stands, record cabinets, instruction books, phonograph needles, inserts for the center holes of 45s, guitar picks, strings and straps, [and] composer statuettes." Nearby, one could shop for pianos, stereos, tape recorders, radios, and televisions. (Courtesy Susan W. Greene.)

Field's wedding registry form not only provided a place for a bride to record her preferences, but also helped her define those preferences, serving as a blueprint for what a bride might need in her new household. This list from the late 1960s includes both casual and formal table settings and such modern "necessities" as a carving set, electric frying pan, hamper, pressure cooker, and television snack tables.

the Bride's preference list
on register at
Marshall Field & Company

THE *Wedding Bureau* | MARSHALL FIELD & COMPANY | CHICAGO

Bride's name ___ Wedding date ___
Address ___ Home Phone ___
City ___ Zone ___ Office Phone ___
Groom's name ___
Future address ___

China Pattern	Has	Needs	Casual Dinnerware	Has	Needs	Stemware Pattern	Has	Needs
Place settings			Place settings			Goblets		
Dinner plates			Dinner plates			Sherbets		
Salad plates			Salad plates			Wines		
Bread and butter plates			Bread and butter plates			Cordials		
Cups & Saucers			Cups & Saucers			Cocktails		
Soup plates, Rim—Cream			Soup plates			Plates		
Fruit dishes			Fruit dishes			Ice Teas		
Platters S——M——L			Cereal bowls					
Vegetable dish			Platters S——M——L——					
Sauce boat			Vegetable dish					
Sugar & Creamer			Divided vegetable bowl					
			Salt & Pepper					
			Sauce boat					
			Sugar & Creamer					
			Butter dish					
			Coffee or Teapot					

Silver Pattern	Has	Needs	Silver Holloware	Has	Needs	Stainless Steel Pattern	Has	Needs
Place settings 4-5-6 Pc.						Place settings 5-6 Pc.		
Knives (size)								
Forks (size)								
Salad forks								
Soup spoons (size)								
Teaspoons						Serving pieces		
Spreaders-Hollow-Flat								
Cocktail forks								
Ice teaspoons								
Tablespoons						Stainless holloware		
Pierced serving spoon								
Gravy ladle								
Sugar spoon								
Butter knife								

ENTERTAINING ACCESSORIES	Needs	TABLE	size	LINENS Colors
Highball glasses		Formal cloth & napkins		
Old fashioneds, single		Luncheon cloth & napkins		
Old fashioneds, double		Place mats		
Cocktails		Bridge cloth & napkins		
Pilsners		BATH		Colors
Cocktail shaker		Towels—bath		
pitcher		—hand		
		—guest		
Ice bucket		Wash cloths		
		Mat sets		
		Bath rugs		
T V snack tables		Shower curtain		
Salad bowl—large		BEDROOM	size	Colors
Salad bowl—individual		Regular flat sheets		
Lazy susan		Contour sheets—top		
Chafing dish		—bottom		
Casserole w/w		Cases		
Serving trays		Blankets—heavy		
		—electrical		
		—summer		
		Bedspreads		
		Comforter		
		Pillows		

Electrical Appliances	Brand	Needs	Kitchen Equipment	Kitchen Accessories
Toaster			Cookware brand	Kitchen tool set
Iron-Steam-Dry			Saucepans 1 qt. 2 qt.	Cutlery set
Mixer-Lge.-Hand			3 qt. 4 qt.	Steak knives
Coffeemaker			Saucepot	Carving set
Waffle iron			Fry pans 8" 10"	Ironing board
Electric fry pan			Double boiler	Canister set
Blender			Dutch oven	
Kitchen clock			Teakettle	Bread box
				Miscellaneous
			Mixing bowls	Card table with chairs
				Lamps
			Pressure cooker	lamps
				Clocks
				Bath scale
				Hamper

Jewelry and specialty stores had established bridal registries earlier, but in 1924, Marshall Field & Company was the first department store to offer one, explaining to customers that a secretary would, "by keeping a list of things sent to each bride, obviate the danger of duplication." It was a win-win situation: brides stood a better chance of receiving gifts they wanted, while the store knew guests would shop at Field's.

The main-aisle decorations for Christmas changed every year. In 1968, enormous, fancifully decorated Christmas trees rose up from the main-aisle display cases. Other years, the decorations featured reindeer carved from "ice," sparkling white frosted trees, or hot air balloons rising up through the rotundas. Virtually all the work for the store's Christmas decorations took place in the 13th-floor studios. When the interior displays and window designs were dismantled, some props and backgrounds went into warehouse storage, while others would be recycled to the branch and shopping center stores. Note that the main floor retained much of its look from the early 1900s, with rounded-corner display cases and enticing impulse goods placed so that shoppers had to pass them en route to the escalators. (Courtesy Chicago History Museum/Gustav D. Frank, ICHi-51200.)

The Christmas box design changed frequently. Photographer and writer James Iska wrote, "The pinnacle of Chicago department stores, Marshall Field's was my mother's domain, she wouldn't set foot in any other store on State Street. My grandmother on the other hand, only went to Field's for the boxes bearing the store's name in which she would wrap the presents she bought at Goldblatt's." The slogan "Store of the Christmas Spirit" dates to 1909.

Older women in fur-trimmed coats shopped the main aisle in 1968. Increasingly known as a store with a dowager clientele, Field's greatest challenge by the late 1960s was attracting younger shoppers. Still, many Chicagoans retained deep emotional ties to the store and its reputation for quality and style, both in fashion and other areas such as home furnishings, remained strong. (Courtesy Chicago History Museum/ Gustav D. Frank, ICHi-51199.)

No feature of the Store for Men struck shoppers as powerfully as the seven-foot-tall stuffed bear in the fifth-floor sports department. Here, the store sold equipment for skiing, fishing, golf, tennis, basketball, sailing, and riding, as well as modern and antique sporting arms. In the years just after World War II, shoppers here could see and purchase an Ercoupe—"America's most advanced airplane." (Courtesy Chicago History Museum/Hedrich-Blessing, HB-32286-a.)

The Store for Men appealed to upper-crust sensibilities by offering everything needed for an outdoor enthusiast's camping vacation along with tailored suits, custom shoes, and designer ties. Still, as chain stores and discount merchandisers proliferated, the Store for Men felt the same pressures as other Field's sections. In 1981, the company moved its men's departments back into the main store and put the building up for sale. (Courtesy Chicago History Museum/Hedrich-Blessing, HB-09478-H.)

The Walnut Room welcomed spring 1969 with a display modeled after Swedish angel chimes. The three-tiered display featured bunnies and child mannequins, with fresh yellow and white tulips encircling the base. The display revolved to glockenspiel-like music. Shoppers anticipating spring holidays could also meet the Easter Bunny in the Walnut Room daily for about a month. (Courtesy Chicago History Museum/ Hedrich-Blessing, HB-32468.)

Models presented a jumpsuit and midi coat ensemble by American designer James Galanos for customers at afternoon showings of the spring designer collections in 1969. Guests at the invitation-only events on March 11 and 12 saw the latest collections modeled on a runway set atop the Walnut Room fountain.

the pacesetter

puts you a step ahead

At Field's in Chicago on Six.
There's nothing like it back home.

Marshall Field & Company

The Pacesetter shop appealed to trendsetters of the late 1960s, with their fur-trimmed coats, wide lapels, and exaggerated hemlines. As specialty boutiques increasingly assumed the role of style arbiter for American shoppers, Marshall Field's fought back, opening trendy boutiques within the store aimed at shoring up its reputation for chic, up-to-the-minute styles.

Field's used hip fashions and contemporary decor to woo young shoppers to the Young Chicago Sportswear section in the early 1970s. Teenagers remained a prime target in the fight to head off the store's reputation as antiquated and old-fashioned. A vigorous, bustling youth department implied that the store as a whole looked and thought young. (Courtesy Chicago History Museum/ Hedrich-Blessing, HB-36563-C.)

Frozen foods, sold from special chilled cabinets, occupied a prominent position in the gourmet food section in 1971. Field's had been among the pioneers in selling frozen foods, introducing frozen groceries at a time when only about 5,000 stores nationwide carried them. For a long time, frozen food appealed only to high-end shoppers who could afford sizeable freezers. (Courtesy Chicago History Museum/Hedrich-Blessing, HB-34518.)

Morning rush-hour commuters arriving at the Randolph Street and Wabash Avenue Loop platform encountered a lighted sign pointing to the store's direct entrance. A similar direct entrance underground permitted passengers arriving via the State Street subway to enter the store immediately, without first accessing the street. The store did everything it could to make it simple for customers to get inside the building. (Courtesy Brian J. Cudahy.)

A Field's sale flier for the 222 line of household goods shows that its range included laundry detergent, paper towels, toilet paper, oven cleaner, and dishwashing detergent. The name 222, pronounced "two-twenty-two," echoed the address of the Merchandise Mart at 222 North Bank Drive (later 222 West Merchandise Mart Plaza). In contrast, the main store used the address 111 State Street.

Schaumburg mayor Robert Atcher (right) and local mover and shaker Ellsworth Meineke helped transform a 191-acre tract into Woodfield Mall. The mall, which was for a while the world's largest indoor shopping center, took its name from Marshall Field and from Robert Wood, chairman of Sears, Roebuck and Company, which was one of the mall's other original 1971 anchors, along with J.C. Penney. (Courtesy Schaumburg Township Historical Society and Schaumburg Township District Library.)

Uncle Mistletoe still appeared in the Christmas windows, as this toy-filled miniature Walnut Room tableau shows, but by the 1970s, his popularity had waned. A new holiday character, Frederick Fieldmouse, was introduced in 1973 and was joined by his wife Marsha in 1977. Friends of Uncle Mistletoe and Aunt Holly, they shared a similar message of kindness at Christmas. (Courtesy Chicago History Museum/Hedrich-Blessing, HB-37765.)

The Crystal Palace Ice Cream Parlour on the third floor evoked the feel of an old-fashioned ice cream shop with its pale pink walls, wire chairs, and stained glass windows. The "paradise in pink and white" sold ice cream made in the store, along with Field's pastries and candies. (Courtesy Chicago History Museum/ Hedrich-Blessing, HB-38956-A.)

The book section remained popular in the early 1970s, even after Field's lost its title of America's largest bookseller (in 1951, it had handled more than a half million transactions and $1.5 million in sales). Under siege from discount and chain bookstores, many department stores had begun eliminating books or reducing stocks to little more than current best sellers and top authors by this time. (Courtesy Chicago History Museum/Hedrich-Blessing, HB-38115-B.)

A **Continental leisure suit** with resort leanings by Izod Ltd. Textured polyester; flap pockets, vents. Natural.
  184-9R-21—regular, 38 to 46, $95.00 ($1.00)
  184-9R-37—long, 40 to 46, $95.00 ($1.00)
Hibiscus print shirt by Grunwald-Marx of DuPont Qiana nylon. Long-sleeve style in brown tones. M, L, XL.
  179-9-23—$28.50 (75¢)
B **Dragon print dress** by DaRue of California. Fluid polyester.
  167-9R-27—multicolor, 8-16, $125.00
C **By Izod Ltd.,** the super suave look in casual attire. Rich, velvety shirt of cotton velour; slacks of polyester gabardine; turtleneck of Dacron polyester/cotton.
  184-9-24—shirt, navy, red or ivory; M, L, XL, $28.50 (85¢)
  184-9-26—slacks, white or navy; 32-40, $30.00 (90¢)
  184-9-25—turtleneck, white, blue; M, L, XL, $14.00 (75¢)
D **Charmingly beached** in coral, by Anne Klein for Penhold. Slip of a maillot in nylon/Lycra spandex. Bell sleeve ombré-stripe coverup; pretty matching sun hat with stitched 8-in. brim. Both polyester/cotton.
  178-9R-30—maillot suit; 6-14, $30.00 (75¢)
  178-9R-31—coverup; S, M, L, $64.00 (85¢)
  178-9R-32—sun hat; one size fits all, $18.00 (75¢)
E **Abstract shapes connected by bead ropes** print up gals pants suit. Beneath, sleeveless red back-zip shell. Sir James puts it together in fluid polyester crepe. Lined pants.
  120-9R-28—pants suit, 8-16, $54.00 (90¢)
  120-9R-29—shell, 8-16, $14.00 (70¢)
F **John Pomer bush style leisure suit** wins admiration at dinner, on vacation, for its great masculine look. Dacron polyester gabardine with epaulets, vents; flared pants. Pale yellow.
  184-9R-34—regular, 38-46, $75.00 ($1.00)
  184-9R-674—long, 40-46, $75.00 ($1.00)
Lion-in-the-bush shirt by Oleg Cassini. Continuous print, front and back. Long sleeved. Nylon. Gold. M, L, XL.
  179-9-33—$30.00 (75¢)
A, C, F, Store for Men; B, Sunningdale®; D, Country Shop; E, Leisure Sportswear

Casual clothing dominated the Field's Christmas catalog of 1975. In this era, stylish designs included fluid, polyester crepe pantsuits and wide-brimmed sun hats for women. Men's offerings included polyester gabardine leisure suits and nylon shirts with vivid prints.

The State Street store might have been almost 14 times bigger, but the Marshall Field's in Water Tower Place (opened October 1975 and seen here in the 1990s) matched it in elegance with parquet floors and marble-sheathed pillars. Water Tower Place's success shifted the economic dynamics of Chicago retail northward. North Michigan Avenue—dubbed the Magnificent Mile—gradually eclipsed State Street as Chicago's premier shopping corridor. (Courtesy Deirdre Woodard, Soulnoir.)

The patchwork craze—inspired by the fashion trends of the early 1970s back-to-nature and hippie movements—found its way to Cozy Cloud Cottage in 1973. Visitors that year found Santa seated inside a cottage decorated with patchwork fabrics and Raggedy Anne dolls. (Courtesy Chicago History Museum/Hedrich-Blessing, HB-37814-A.)

A Chinese magician performed for children at the 1975 employee Christmas party. For many Field's workers and their children, the holiday season kicked off with the annual event, held on an early December Sunday in the Walnut Room. Employees and their children could also meet Santa and enjoy punch, eggnog, butter cookies, and desserts.

Children at the 1975 party also made wishes with the Fairy Princess, a long-running part of Christmas at Field's for customers. Typically, she went from table to table in the Walnut Room. "I would walk around wearing a giant pink prom dress and some wings and sprinkle fairy dust on kids while they made Christmas wishes," recalled actress Stephanie March, who worked as the Fairy Princess years later, in the 1990s.

In anticipation of the national bicentennial, the craze for all things Colonial hit the main aisle for Christmas 1975. Decorations that year consisted of faux building facades set up around the main aisle columns featuring various Colonial-style shops. Note the stools for customers trying on hats. (Courtesy Chicago History Museum/ Hedrich-Blessing, HB-39877-C.)

Step Back In Time

Footnotes to history: Commemorating the Bicentennial, Marshall Field & Company proudly presents a sampling of significant American papers and artware, from our collections of unique manuscripts and antique pewter. All subject to prior sale.

A Autographed letter signed by John Jay, President of the Continental Congress, first Chief Justice. 11 pages, quarto, Bedford, April 15, 1818 to John Murray, Jr., discussing whether war is forbidden by the Bible. One of the longest, most interesting and important letters of John Jay extant. Bound in full crimson morocco, gilt.
199-9R-3—$12,500.00

B From George Washington, a magnificent autograph letter, signed. One page, folio with integral address leaf. From headquarters at Springfield, June 20, 1780, to Robert Morris and B. McClenachan, Merchants. A superb letter reaffirming his devotion to the cause of independence. With an engraved portrait and transcript.
199-9R-4—$12,000.00

C Window ledge sundial by Josiah Miller of New England, circa 1725-1775. Holes show where it was nailed to sill, so owner could gauge time. 4½ inches; marked.
199-9R-4—in red half-morocco slipcase, $8,500.00

D Pewter porringer by Frederick Bassett of New York City and Hartford, Conn., circa 1761-1800. A rarity, one of the few extant pieces by this maker. Marked, 5-inch diameter.
199-9R-6—$4,500.00

E Pewter dinner plate by William Will of Philadelphia who served as a colonel in the Revolutionary War. Nine-inch plate, made between 1764-1798, has Will's touchmark.
302-9R-5—$5,000.00

F Broad-rim plate by Edmund Dolbeare, circa 1690-1711, one of the earliest pewterers in America, who worked in Boston or Salem. Touch-marked, 13-inch diameter.
302-9R-6—$12,000.00

G A Plan of the Operations of the King's Army under the command of Gen. Howe in New York and East New Jersey, against the American Forces commanded by Gen. Washington. London, Faden, Feb. 25, 1777. Pictorial news of the war was limited almost entirely to maps. This is one of the most detailed, accurate and informative revolutionary war battle plans showing the movements of both armies. Handsomely framed. 28¾ x 19 inches.
199-9R-7—$1,100.00

A, B, G, Antiquarian Book, Map and Print Room; C-F, Antique Pewter

For those wanting to own some Colonial history, the store offered a framed Revolutionary War map from 1777 ($1,100) and broad-rim pewter plate ($12,000). Like the $300 lace shawl offered in 1868 and the $800 tablecloth in the 1890s, these prestige pieces served mostly to grab attention and bolster the store's reputation for unique merchandise. Most bicentennial enthusiasts probably satisfied themselves with reproduction candlesticks ($25) or a bicentennial calendar ($4.95).

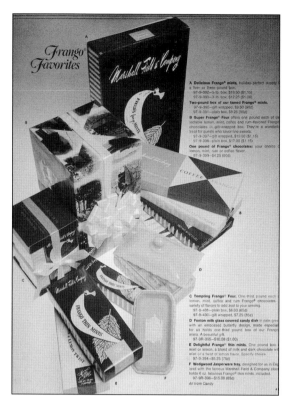

By 1975, Frango mints were a firmly established Marshall Field's tradition, showcased here on a full-page Christmas catalog spread in all four flavors: lemon, mint, coffee, and rum. By 1998, Marshall Field's (and then owner Dayton Hudson) would be selling some 1.2 million pounds of Frangoes for $14 a pound in flavors such as mint, raspberry, caramel, toffee, and double chocolate as well as permutations such as coffee, cocoa, cookies, and liqueurs.

Between 1974 and 1977, the company poured $6 million into remodeling the main floor, long considered hallowed. The remodeling acknowledged that Field's and other department stores were feeling the pinch as luxury emporia from outside Chicago such as Saks Fifth Avenue and I. Magnin opened along Michigan Avenue's Magnificent Mile. The remodeled candy section shows the modern fixtures and new emphasis on self service. (Courtesy Chicago History Museum/Hedrich-Blessing, HB-41754.)

Five

NEW OWNERSHIP, NEW DIRECTIONS

(1982–2001)

The main floor glittered at Christmas 1985, but to many, Field's image needed polishing and its approach needed updating. In an attempt to fend off takeovers, the company had purchased chains in various parts of the country, including Texas, Florida, California, North Carolina, Ohio, and Oregon. When BATUS Inc., the US arm of British tobacco firm B.A.T. Industries, purchased the 22-unit Marshall Field's chain in 1982 for $367 million, the Chicago division was in a slump. (Courtesy David Wilson.)

The store's long-running tradition of spectacular promotions continued with the launch of The Eagle and The Crown in September 1986. This four-month promotion of all things British featured tea-making demonstrations, shortbread tastings, British specialty foods and gifts, a visit from the great-grandson of Charles Dickens, and a miniature model of the Duchess of Devonshire's drawing room. The Prince of Wales stopped by to launch the promotion.

The Myers family visited Marshall Field's every year from 1979 to 1997. Christy Myers explains, "Such fun days those were! We'd dress up, go to Field's with my parents to see Santa, then have ice cream in the Crystal Palace and head home. We're down in Ottawa, so it was an hour and a half drive, each way." (Courtesy the Steve and Christy Myers Family, 1989.)

Joining the long list of fashion icons who visited the State Street store, renowned Italian fashion designer Valentino stopped by in 1986 to hand out samples of his new fragrance and photographs of himself. But all was not sparkling at Marshall Field's. The Evanston and Oak Park branches closed after the 1986 holiday season, and the men's departments had recently been moved back into the main building. In downtown Chicago, stores up and down State Street closed in the 1980s, including Chas. A. Stevens, Goldblatt's, Montgomery Ward, the original Sears, and Wieboldt's. Attempts to boost retail sales and curb attrition by transforming the shopping area into a transit mall failed to stop the decline. Where shopping emporia had once stretched for blocks, by 1990 only Carson Pirie Scott and Marshall Field's remained.

New owner BATUS found the main floor's look jarring, with chrome display cases and modern light fixtures that clashed against the store's original Corinthian columns. BATUS soon announced plans for a $115-million renovation to overhaul the store's look and its merchandise. The five-year renovation project began in 1987. (Courtesy Chicago Loop Alliance and Chicago Public Library, Special Collections and Preservations Division, Chicago Loop Alliance Collection, 7/17 [2].)

Renovators updated the main floor by installing wooden display cases reminiscent of the originals and new dropped ceiling panels, which kept the store's original ceiling moldings and Corinthian columns intact, but accommodated modern air conditioning and sprinklers. Recessed lighting around the edges bounced light up to the now-gilded column capitals. (Courtesy Chicago Loop Alliance and Chicago Public Library, Special Collections and Preservations Division, Chicago Loop Alliance Collection, 7/17 [2].)

Before the renovation, displays of children's clothing on the fourth floor looked tired and outdated. The flooring and fixtures lacked the colorful zip common in mega toy stores and children's clothing boutiques by this time. (Courtesy Chicago Loop Alliance and Chicago Public Library, Special Collections and Preservations Division, Chicago Loop Alliance Collection, 7/17 [3].)

The renovation relocated the children's department to the fifth floor and added stimulating modern visual effects. Colorful floor patterning, asymmetrical merchandising displays, and modern lighting better positioned the store as a home for fashion-forward children's clothing. (Courtesy Chicago Loop Alliance and Chicago Public Library, Special Collections and Preservations Division, Chicago Loop Alliance Collection, 7/17 [3].)

At the heart of the renovation stood an 11-story, 165-foot-high atrium with a backlit barrel-vaulted "skylight." The area had formerly been an airshaft and alley that, for decades, forced customers to walk outside to travel between the Wabash Avenue and State Street sections. The atrium finally solved this annoyance and unsnarled longstanding traffic circulation problems caused by firewalls, look-alike escalators, and piecemeal modernization. (Courtesy Thomas Fitzgerald, 2005.)

Signs announced the new floor-by-floor merchandise arrangements, which most notably included the move of children's merchandise to the fifth floor and the end of the lower level as a bargain floor. As always, the store continued tweaking departments, gradually adding more boutiques. The early 2000s saw the addition of boutiques for British clothing designer Thomas Pink, New York home designer Thomas O'Brian, and Internet giant Yahoo! (Courtesy Galen R. Frysinger.)

The renovation also brought the north light well back to its original splendor. Workers restored the skylight and removed metal screens that had barricaded the upper-floor openings for decades. According to store legend, the screens were installed after a man leaped to his death following the 1929 stock market crash. (Courtesy Galen R. Frysinger.)

The atrium soon became a popular meeting spot. Visible here behind the perfume counters is a six-ton, cast-iron fountain cascading with close to 700 gallons of water. Researchers preparing for the renovations had uncovered drawings for the fountain in the original store plans from D.H. Burnham & Company. Marshall Field had nixed the idea, but the fountain was finally built in 1992. (Courtesy Galen R. Frysinger.)

Water hoses snaked out of the store on April 17, 1992, pumping brownish river water from the basement. Four days earlier, a drill had accidently punched into pipes under the Chicago River, flooding an ancient freight tunnel system under the Loop and shutting down businesses for months. The flood hit Field's hard, pouring water into the two lower sub-basements. The store defied expectations by partially reopening just one week later. With water still sloshing in the lowest basements and the restaurants closed, Mayor Richard M. Daley greeted cheering employees. Although the heating and electrical systems would not be fully restored for months, the store's remarkably quick recovery, along with the makeover of State Street Mall in 1996 and the reopening of the byway to automobile traffic, brought renewed optimism to State Street. (Courtesy Associated Press/Mark Elias.)

Six

END OF AN ERA
(2002–2006)

An enormous American flag, first unfurled on Memorial Day 2003, stretched down the north light well from the eighth to second floors. Most gaping spectators probably never knew that it was the third flag hung in this location. The first, a 900-pound, 50-by-100-foot behemoth commissioned in 1916, was hung every Memorial Day and Fourth of July for 25 years. The second, unveiled in 1942, was displayed through 1945. (Courtesy Gillian Troup.)

The company shattered a Guinness World Record when it unveiled the world's largest box of chocolates in 2002. The fifteen-by-seven-foot box held 2,002 one-pound boxes of Frango Mints (90,000 candies in all) and kicked off the second year of a promotion called the Frango Win-a-Mint game. The candies were later donated to local charities and non-profits. Marshall Field's Guinness record stood until 2008. (Courtesy the Maccabee Group, Inc.)

The wildly popular Frango candies led to restaurant and bakery spin-offs, including mint chocolate chip cookies, Frango chocolate cheesecake, and, most popular of all, Frango mint ice cream pie. Store cookbooks gave fans instructions for creating their own version, complete with graham cracker crust, homemade Frango ice cream, and a hazelnut praline topping. (Courtesy Terawaki Kawamoto.)

A chef's hat topped the famous clock to promote the launch of the *Marshall Field's Cookbook*. The store also opened a 4,200-square-foot culinary studio in 2004 and hosted frequent food-themed special events. For many, though, the era's biggest Field's food story stemmed from then-owner Dayton Hudson's decision in 1999 to move all Frango production to Pennsylvania. Some Frango manufacturing returned to Chicago in 2009. (Courtesy Alexandra Constantin.)

The Walnut Room children's menu for the holidays in 2005 reflected modern tastes: pizza, cheeseburgers, and chicken fritters. Children received drinks in limited-edition souvenir Santabear mugs and could order a cookie decorated as Santabear. The Santabear promotion, centered on a stuffed white teddy bear dressed in different garb each holiday season, was launched in 1985 and lasted 23 years.

WALNUT ROOM CHILDREN'S MENU

$7.95

CHICKEN FRITTERS crispy breaded chicken tenderloins with choice of French fries or applesauce

OOEY GOOEY PIZZA tender crust with tomato sauce and mozzarella cheese

MAC AND CHEESE elbow macaroni with creamy mild cheddar cheese sauce

MINI CORN DOGS with choice of French fries or applesauce

CHEESEBURGER, with choice of French fries or applesauce

Each meal includes choice of beverage and a souvenir limited-edition 2005 Marshall Field's Santabear mug, while quantities last.

CHILDREN'S HOLIDAY DESSERTS

$3.50

SANTABEAR COOKIE

ICE CREAM SNOWMAN

Wally and Victor, costumed elf characters from Those Funny Little People, drew a large following in their annual appearances during the holidays beginning in 1980. When the Field's manager who first hired them, Janet Connor, retired in the early 1990s, Wally and Victor (along with their siblings, Mr. Mint and Miss Sample) showed up for her send-off. (Courtesy Those Funny Little People Enterprises, Inc.)

Crowds packed the grounds outside the store in September 2003 for a spectacular vertical fashion show, which featured athlete models who, suspended by cables, descended a runway extending from roof to sidewalk. Here, Carolina Olumfemi models clothing by designer Thomas Pink as she walks down the building. (Courtesy Associated Press/Anne Ryan.)

Triumphant gilded horns heralded the arrival of Christmas on State Street. Amy Meadows, senior manager of windows and marketing events at Marshall Field's, designed the horns as much for practicality as for visual flair. "Like the famed snowflakes which preceded them, they needed to incorporate the flagpoles," she explained. The banners hanging from them were engineered so that fierce winter winds would move through—not against—them. (Courtesy Heather L. Kribs.)

The 2005 holiday windows featured the story of Cinderella. For many Chicago families, seeing the Marshall Field's Christmas windows was a cherished annual tradition. Blogger Danny Miller wrote, "Who doesn't remember their first trip downtown to see the magical Christmas windows at Field's? In my house, this event was anticipated with the same excitement as the annual TV viewing of *The Wizard of Oz*." (Courtesy Samadhi Metta Bexar.)

More than 300 protestors, some in costume, gathered on September 9, 2007, to mark the one-year anniversary of the store's rebranding as Macy's (250 had shown up in 2006). They were protesting what they felt was the loss of part of Chicago's civic identity. Macy's acknowledged their grief, but countered that cost-efficient modern business practice called for a single name, enabling the retailer to streamline marketing and leverage national advertising for its 800-plus stores. (Courtesy Timothy State.)

Today, the building operates as Macy's on State Street, one of Macy's four specialized flagship stores. It was named a National Historic Landmark in 1978 and a Chicago Landmark in 2005. The clocks, the Walnut Room, the Christmas tree, Frango mints, and the corner plaques remain, as do memories of, what was for many, a place where nothing was impossible and dreams came true. (Courtesy Thomas Miller, 2006.)

BIBLIOGRAPHY

Ditchett, S.H. *Marshall Field & Company: The Life Story of a Great Concern*. New York: Dry Goods Economist, 1922.

Greene, Joan. *A Chicago Tradition: Marshall Field's Food and Fashion*. Petaluma, CA: Pomegranate, 2005.

Howard, Vicki. *Brides, Inc.: American Weddings and the Business of the Tradition*. Philadelphia: University of Pennsylvania Press, 2006.

Kimbrough, Emily. *Through Charley's Door*. New York: Harper and Brothers, 1952.

Koehn, Nancy F. *Brand New: How Entrepreneurs Earned Consumers' Trust from Wedgwood to Dell*. Boston: Harvard Business School Press, 2001.

Leach, William. *Land of Desire: Merchants, Power, and the Rise of New American Culture*. New York: Vintage Books, 1993.

Ledermann, Robert P. *Chicago's State Street Christmas Parade*. Charleston, SC: Arcadia Publishing, 2004.

———. *Christmas on State Street: 1940s and Beyond*. Charleston, SC: Arcadia Publishing, 2002.

Longstreth, Richard. *The American Department Store Transformed: 1920–1960*. New Haven and London: Yale University Press, 2010.

Marshall Field & Company. *Marshall Field's Frango Chocolate Cookbook*. Chicago and New York: Contemporary Books, 1988.

Pridmore, Jay. *Marshall Field's (A Building Book)*. Petaluma, CA: Pomegranate, 2002.

Siegelman, Stephen. *The Marshall Field's Cookbook: Classic Recipes and Fresh Takes from the Field's Culinary Council*. San Francisco: Book Kitchen, 2006.

Twyman, Robert W. *History of Marshall Field & Co., 1852–1906*. Philadelphia: University of Pennsylvania Press, 1954.

Wendt, Lloyd and Herman Kogan. *Give the Lady What She Wants! The Story of Marshall Field & Company*. Chicago, New York, and San Francisco: Rand McNally and Company, 1952.

Whitaker, Jan. *Service and Style: How the American Department Store Fashioned the Middle Class*. New York: St. Martin's Press, 2006.

Discover Thousands of Local History Books
Featuring Millions of Vintage Images

Arcadia Publishing, the leading local history publisher in the United States, is committed to making history accessible and meaningful through publishing books that celebrate and preserve the heritage of America's people and places.

Find more books like this at
www.arcadiapublishing.com

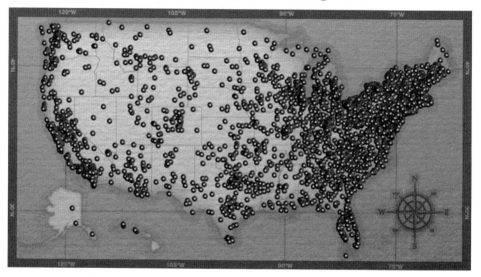

Search for your hometown history, your old stomping grounds, and even your favorite sports team.

Consistent with our mission to preserve history on a local level, this book was printed in South Carolina on American-made paper and manufactured entirely in the United States. Products carrying the accredited Forest Stewardship Council (FSC) label are printed on 100 percent FSC-certified paper.